POETIC CHOCOLATE

Poetry, prose, and short stories

by

Gina Batie

Gina Batie

12/07

authorHOUSE®

AuthorHouse™
1663 Liberty Drive, Suite 200
Bloomington, IN 47403
www.authorhouse.com
Phone: 1-800-839-8640

First published by AuthorHouse 10/22/2007

ISBN: 978-1-4343-1651-6 (sc)

Printed in the United States of America
Bloomington, Indiana

This book is printed on acid-free paper.

POETIC CHOCOLATE

Spiritual Espresso with Motivational Mocha

Chocolate Molds
Poetry and prose for students and teachers

Cocoa Beans
Poetry and prose for children

Pure Chocolate
Poetry and prose for social awareness

Hot Chocolate

Love poems

Solid Chocolate

Poetry, prose and short stories for and about men

Mocha Lace

Poetry and prose for women

Assorted Sweets
Families
Poetry, prose and short stories

Chocolate Shavings
Relationships
Poetry, prose and short stories

Chocolate Ink
Poetry and prose for poets and writers

SPIRITUAL ESPRESSO WITH MOTIVATIONAL MOCHA

His Song

When I was just about to give
up I heard the Lord he said "My
promises are real"

Don't give up! Don't give up!
I gave you all those dreams
At the weakest points in your
 life I've never left it seems

Give the Lord his glory
Continue to praise
Your wondrous blessings are
coming
And all will amazed
I've sacrificed my life
You're encountering strife

At my weakest point I can hear
him say
I've given you all
Sometimes you will do some
running but before that you
must crawl

Don't give up! Don't give up!
God is still here
Your path may be cloudy
Directions unclear
Don't give up! Don't give up!

I can hear my savior say
I am on this journey with you,
you are on my pathway

I love you don't you give up
I made you you're my child
The pain you have inside you it
last only a while

I love you don't you give up

I have something for you
Be open to receive
You can do all things through
Christ Jesus with him you'll
Achieve

Thank you Lord! Oh thank you
For the love you've given me
At my darkest hours your
Promises, I'm still able to see

You love me unconditionally
Your promises are kept
And through it al oh Lord you
haven't left me yet

Thank You Lord! Oh Thank
You!

Your Victory

As every snowflake is different so are life's problems.
Snowflakes fall and compound ....mounds of distress take hold coldness numbs your insides.
Pain is powerful.

It's the heaviness of the icy weights pulling your heart down into the depths of a fearful fighting frenzy.
Fighting for survival... fighting for relief ...a fight towards light.
A light that will heat the icy issues of life.

My soul is caught up in a chain of thorny issues that prick my faith and bleeds towards my Lord.
I come to him on my knees with pleas,
Please Lord deliver me for I cannot see an end to the massacre of my future yet I know that you will deliver me and I know that you are still here and I know I should not fear yet I do and you have never left me for I cannot see my tomorrows.

Pressures rise and I can only think of an end ......the period .....some closure .....
relief....a retreat ....a complete eraser of past problems would not be best.
My lesson is to carry my faith and rest.

I'll hang in there I know that you have prepared a place for me.
In the midst of my journey I couldn't see
But you've always come; you've set me free.

We swagger through life as though we feel that certain things shouldn't happen to us
Well, life happens.

Stand strong.... hold tight ....win the fight!

Stand strong..... hold tight ...win the fight!

Your soul becomes pollen spores blowing in the wind seemingly without direction....
seemingly without protection but remember God created that wind and the spores, too.
He has a destination for each and every one of them and he has a destination for you, too
.....don't give up until he's through....molding, creating, displaying.

There's greatness at the end of that journey,
This will be your testimony,
This will be what others will see to strengthen their walk to victory.

Never Give Up On Your Dreams

Never give up on your dreams, Never give up on your dreams,
I said never give up on your dreams!

You've entered the land of Hope For Your Future.

There will be many moments of stress
That's what occurs on hiking trips where the destination is success,
Keep in mind your vision is blessed
He's the director of this business quest.

Surround yourself with good people who share your vision.
Ask for God's light when making decisions.

There's a wilderness of fear for the unknown,
Paths of doubting undertones.
There's that heat of those outstanding loans.
It's your sheer determination and backbone.

Stress with deadlines,
Fulfillment in personal designs,
Inevitable times to shine.

Encounters with nay sayers the heat of critics,
Never give up on your dreams stay with it!

Take chances, mountains are there to climb
You'll reach the top in His time.

Remember this,
No's are not dead ends
Simply God's compass, His redirections
The Holy Spirits protections
Life's "meant to be" lessons.

Had you not gone through it,
You would've never knew it.

Draw strength in knowing who you are and whose you are
And just this attempt right here makes you the superstar
NEVER GIVE UP ON YOUR DREAMS!

4

Angel of Perspective

When I get up in the morning and my hair won't go just right
My car needs gas I forgot to fill it last night
I burnt my toast and now I don't have my complete breakfast
I remember my Angel of Perspective.

You see she be losing her hair as chemicals are pumped into her to keep her alive and I'll
survive…. burnt toast and a bad hair day
But today her childhood play
May be interrupted with a trip to save her life.

She becomes disfigured like molding clay as the steroid laced needles are shot into her
Her bones ache as a result of just one more shot into her spine….
she's only nine
 But she never complained
And her mother cries silent tears as she reflects on her child's life.

How long will she live?
How much can they give,
to make her better?

I'm upset though because I can't find my keys this morning and I've ripped yet another
contact lense….. mo' money, mo' money.

Can mo' money buy Sarah her health?
Can mo' money provide her parents Spiritual Wealth?

She be my Angel of Perspective because every time there's no one sitting where she
should be that day
I realize my life isn't the best but if my
Angel of Perspective can adjust
Surely I can get over it.

So the next time you're late,
The cashier has a problem and you've got to wait
Take the time to get your perspective straight

And

Remember my Angel of Perspective.

Imprisoned

Sleeping on a carpet of talent that nothing outside your small, empty one room psychological prison will see
No ambitions, no goals nor thoughts of where you should be

Your mind is fed low leveled living and hopeless choices and the negative voices have penetrated your daily devotions to The Most High

You continue to feed your spirit spoiled fruit
Weakening pursuits

No love given, No love received
Just an old flea infested negative mind set, laced with samples of all the times you've tried something and it didn't work
Determined now not to exert any effort towards preparing yourself for your blessings

Don't allow life's tics to suck the ambition from your goals,
infecting the inner core of your sole

Don't give up on the windows of infinite opportunistic skies
Endless questioning of why, why me?
Why not you?
Just heating a large pot to stew in.
Don't make a bed of misgivings,
Sip the fruit juices of failure for breakfast,
Chew on not being chosen,
Garnish life's plates with powerless potential,
Then serve up self pity for desert

Your main entry; complaints and hopelessness served up on a bed of countless misconceptions about life's process
Embrace whatever God gives you, you are still blessed

Try devouring the deserts of determination
Lavishing in the unlimited lessons learned
Continue on your character building quest
And consume the compassion that God was shaping you for all along

Spirits Garment

When you take your garments off at night and lay with another does God see you?

When you put it on in the morning is it just to cover up what's there?
Is it to shield a sinner's glare?
Is it to cover embarrassing, private, wicked moments performed under magnetic moonlit skies?
Is it worn to cover the naked lies?
Is it to muffle the torturous cries, of those you've destroyed with your soiling tongue?

Do you place your garments on just to impress Reverend Ohsogood and the sanctified sisters of the St. Tabernacle choir?
Do you wear those garments to cover the fact that you're really a liar?

Your spirit is a saturation of your soul, it's a complete painting of you
It's not a garment.
God has a way of straightening out our wrinkles with some heat.
Ironing and pressing
Starching, undressing

When you willfully soil the garments
of others with your hoity secretions of stains and tarnish.
Don't do it in the name of Jesus.

While the sick and down trodden ask for help
And you with your selfish sanctimonious self.
Front as though you've never been there
While giving them your self righteous stare.

Because it's only God's grace and mercy that keeps you
And he kept you here and saw you through.

When your clothes are tattered and torn
And your soul is stretched and worn.

Thank God because he has a forgiving heart
Thank Him because he's willing to clean, iron out, firm up our lives and give us all a fresh start.

Life Notes

As my life became
a kaleidoscope of
fragmented colorful
pieces on display
As an audience glared at
the filmography within
my soul
Tiny excerpts of hurt,
pain and embarrassment
became jocular
ammunition from the
losels of life
Those losels besmear my
guts and lubricate them
with self doubt
Which one of you will
participate in the
holocaust of my zeal?
Enter into this oasis of
various hues chosen by
the author herself and
become the quagmire
that causes me to lose
my grip?

You see it's not that I
am irreproachable
but I refuse to allow the
epitome of what I never
want to become to
immigrate within my
drive, my presence, my
strength
Lock my innovational
ability into the cells
buried beneath their
absence of successful
ventures
And as a nationalist
locate the gherkins of
the poetic parklands
within me

They need to relieve
themselves with an
orgasm of personal
assessment
They realize that the
armor of my swaying
silk dress or my holey
jeans and tennis shoes
don't make me The
Madonna nor a Kaiser
I am still able to
flamenco at the Party of
Life because I am a true
writer of verse

CHOCOLATE MOLDS

Poetry and prose for students and teachers

Teacher's Pledge

Being a teacher is like harvesting lives

When you touch it, it shows
When you nurture it, it grows
And when you love it, it knows

I am a teacher
A giver of knowledge
A pusher of potential
A lover of little lives

My high is their success
My dreams are their best
My life- Endless dedication
A builder of nations
I AM A TEACHER

My rewards are the high I get when they blossom
The self-esteem that rises because my method is to soak those lives with an "I am beautiful belief"
And it doesn't matter what they really look like as long as they think highly of themselves
As long as they know they have value and potential… it's essential to their success

Negative spirits will tear at their worth
And I know that they've been issued tremendous challenges placed at their birth

But we have the power, power to create scientist, inventors, presidents, professors, leaders, teachers and independent thinkers

Because a teacher understands that their circumstances don't determine their altitude
Their circumstances are what I'm going to use to instill determination and self-discipline
They can win
Because their obstacles are to be successful battles, strengthening tools to use

Elevating these seeds are a fight to be fought and a battle to be won

Their circumstances will not be an excuse for failure

Their circumstances today will not dictate what their tomorrows will be
Because I see
Achievement in those troubled places

I see greatness in those little faces

Dear Teacher,

I came to you all tattered and torn
Of your criticism I was not forewarned

I left my house excited to learn
My spirit experienced a very slow burn

She said, "Boy where is your other shoe lace?"
Well ma'am I was late for the bus so I hastened
my pace.

See I got myself ready today
My grandma was in bed and still there she'd lay

I wanted to learn what Mrs. Smith had to say
So I dressed myself and made my way
She reminded me of my mother who died last
year
My memories of mom are still very clear
Boy, what happened to your clothes?
I'm only six years here and this is how it goes,
Grandma was busy late last night
I got myself dressed, maybe not quiet right

Like a dart board dodging an intended prick of
 my spirit
dance with words that hope will save me.
"Uhm, Uh please don't embarrass me I wanted
to come to school
I'm out of uniform, I'm breaking an important
rule
But I want to learn
Your knowledge I seek
Now my heart is heavy, I'm trying not to weep
And with your nurturing, I may turn out to be
A good man
So I'll hold my head high and before you I'll
stand
Seeking your knowledge
Sapping up your intellect so I too can attend
college

My background doesn't matter, it isn't the very best
But I am on a journey, a complicated quest

I'm trying to rise above poverty
Surpass generations before me
I hope you really do see
The man your helping me to be
So the next time you have a problem with what I
am wearing
The next time you get tired and believe it's
easier to stop caring

My background doesn't matter, it isn't the very best
But I am on a journey, complicated quest
Seeking your knowledge,
Sapping up your intellect so I too can attend
college
I need you to guide me, I haven't been taught
This is the plight I've been issued and in the
lack of intellectuality I'm temporarily caught

I can change and I can be molded
I'm still very young
I'm still a little rowdy and quite high strung
But you can care enough to mold me well
You can take the time to blaze my trail

I'll remember you always, as the person who
made me
I'll remember you always as the person who
taught me to see
Beyond my reality
And into a successful future
So thank you dear teacher for ignoring my
tattered clothes, not turning up your nose
And just molding me"

Thank you love always,
Success

COCOA BEANS

Poetry and prose for children

I Don't Know What Page We're On

Okay class turn to page 29 in your math books, today we're learning about blah ... blah... blah.....blah
As I daydream about what mom packed in my lunch
My stomach growls, good thing I snuck that extra bag of Crunch and Munch

As I think about throwing this spit wad at my best friend Johnny who at least looks like he's paying attention
I know his mind is in another dimension
Because we brought our super new Sponge Bob Square Pants action figures in our new backpacks
And a small bag of Yahoos for a secret classroom snack.

As I contemplate faking the hiccups so everyone will stop and look at me
And I get that wonderful opportunity
to leave the classroom alone headed for Hallway Heaven
Next door in room eleven
I peak at Lisa who was in Mrs. Smith's class with me last year.
And look into Mr. Ramirez's room at Chester whose picking his ears.
And Billy I'm glad he's not in my class anymore
Last year, he stole my lunch money and left me in fear.

I go to Miss Batie and ask her to go to the restroom for the 10th additional time because
"Miss Batie, my stomach hurts"
I prayed to God for another fire alarm alert
That didn't happen
Sally picks her buggers and grosses me out

Now I have no idea what Miss Batie's talking about
Carl created a new sound with his armpits and amazed the entire class except Miss Batie.
Miss Batie begins, "Pinellapie! I jump, What's the answer?"
"Oh, Uh teacher I don't know what page we're on.

Do You Know Who You Are?

Do you know who you are?
You are Nefertiti whose name means the beautiful one has come
Daughter of the Gods
Empress of the Mediterranean
Definition of Style
Ruler of the Nile

You are Mekeda the Legendary Queen of Sheba
Mekeda the Beautiful as she was known
You, you my children are placed highest on the throne

You defeated Asian invaders you are Menes the first Pharaoh of a United Egypt
Truth of history from our sweet nectar they've sipped

You are the various hues of music ... rhythm ...rhymes

Creators of black words on white pages with colorful lines

You are afro puffs, corn rolls, braids, twists and dreadlocks
You are the walk with a smooth stride
You are the creator of the Four Corners, Bump, Harlem Shake and Electric Slide

You are Percy Julian, the scientist who saved thousands of servicemen in World War II
with an invention
For you not to know is the world's intention
Your history books continuously conveniently failed to mention

You are strength and
What you've been taught .....ain't

You are the salt that adds flavor to the earth
You are the beginning ...the world's birth

Where others want to be you- They dream
You are chocolate, caramel, mahogany, licorice, the coffee in our cream
Our African Kings and Queens
You are Joseph Lee inventor of the bread making and bread crumbing machine
You are, You are a black pearl more precious than gold
Our bodies were sold
Inferior we're told
Your dignity, beauty and strength is taxed but not controlled
Truth must unfold...
Stand and be bold .....
Because baby you are more precious than gold

Ginae

The source of my poetry is...
My niece sitting on my dad's lap feeding chirping seagulls near the ocean

The source of my poetry is...
In her sparkling smile while grabbing French fries from her plate

My poetry is in the development of the beautiful sounds she makes, not quite words but soothing melodies of gestures and meaningful demands

The source of my poetry.....
Is that flowery, lacey dress worn at Easter

It's in the funny faces she makes

The source of my poetry is running her bath water and observing the joy in her eyes for the bubbles...that only her baby faced beauty could capture

The source of my poetry is her sassy movements when one of her favorite songs comes on the radio

And yes I pour into her
waterfalls of intellectuality, fountains of morality pitchers of peace
Because I know what it's like to be a specimen under insecurities microscope
I know what it's like to be analyzed constantly
To feel that love was always conditional

To be made to feel as though I was less than everyone around me
only because they knew who I was...a prized jewel, a beautiful gift

Someone said to me, Hispanic children are so beautiful and they are...So I would like to add that kinks and midnight black, wavy and caramel tan, snow white and straight are the creations of the creator ...So whatever Markoiya Ginae Batie is, it's all good

Wasted years
Life's growth tears
Silent cheers....FROM THEM

Today I know why, who, what and how
And baby it's now
IT'S MY TIME! IT'S
HER TIME!

She won't endure the
wasted years I've spent not knowing

Afraid of showing

Because I didn't want anyone to think that I thought I was better than them
But I'm full to the brim baby....
I'm full of self
Spiritual Wealth
My challenge to everyone tonight is to get some
Allow yourself to become Full of Spiritual Wealth

Because she is the very essence of my poetry
AND
I see insecurities microscope attempting to devalue The Source of My Poetry

Blue Black and Beautiful

He was blue black and beautiful
Dark like the night sky, peppered with stars of promise
A New Orleans native
Flushed out like a fish from his home
He was spicy and fiesty straight out of the Fisher Projects

Working hard the product of a system that has supplied low expectations
Low income and low living
The haves will continue to have and the have nots will have not for generations to come

Thrust into a system of opposites he struggles to survive
He has systematically been kept ignorant
With boo coos of ability yet obviously far behind most his peers here

He was blue black , He was beautiful, An African Prince
A 6 year old street professional
A survivor

Respectful to his elders
while demanding respect from his peers
Grown beyond his 6 years
Always ready to make one of his classmates dollars disappear

Magic tricks, let's see if we can make his poverty disappear... a mirky path is ahead for the
blue black prince
And since most of us don't care.... where will he be when we multiply his 6 years by 3
Will he just be seen as an object to throw away
or will we start right now and use our resources to mold my blue black baby like clay?

He was blue black and beautiful
Dark like the night sky, peppered with promise

PURE CHOCOLATE

Poetry and prose for social awareness

My Fare Lady

London Bridges falling down, falling down, falling down, London Bridges falling down, my fare lady

You see her bridge to success was her need for others to build up in her what she never got at home...love....unconditional love

She thought she'd find it in the back seat of the car of the first boy that showed her any attention
She thought it was in the cat calls she got when she dressed half naked
She thought it was in that old man giving her money and telling her she was beautiful

London Bridges falling down... down

When he came to her and told her she could make some money with those looks
She was thinking modeling, video dancer, he was thinking motels and resale
Yea baby I can make you a star
Get you off that bus and into a new car

That pimp didn't tell her that her soul would be festered with S. T. D.' s
While own her knees
Trying to please
A man old enough to be her grandfather

He didn't tell her that in just months that youthful beauty would turn to dried up weary tomorrows and dead end dreams
All that was important was what was between her legs and what he was passing out wasn't love and opportunity cards
What he was passing out was degradation and death tickets

Take the key and lock her up, lock her up ....Lock her up

The glitz and glamour
Have now turned to tricks and clamor
The clamor of the bars shutting behind her and that pimp who got her started now beats her and pumps her full of drugs

Men get in line right here to find the soul of your African Queen
Get in line to dim the shine
Of her youthful giggles and adolescent zest
Get in line right here to degrade the birth mother of earth's life
Get in line to kill and steal our future

She was never told
She didn't know this world could be so cold
That she was selling her sole
That her life would unfold like this

Love your children and let them know openly that everyone makes mistakes
The mistake doesn't define them..
They never become the mistake

My Fare Lady

Mother Africa

Africa, Mother Africa
Your winds are my breath to breathe
Your spirit my strength to continue

Africa, Mother Africa
I long to till your soil of sick souls
I long to run free in my very own blessed community
Free from hate, free from fear.... Free
Free to love, free to direct our children towards that pure spirit of righteousness
Your beauty abounds above all others
You are nature, you are gold and diamonds
You are black coal and white ivory
You are green mountains and blue rivers

Africa, Mother Africa you have given birth to these words may they grow into mature
expansions of knowledge
May they marry wisdom and spread strength's off springs throughout the land that once
was home for us

Changes in Chocolate Notes

I remember when music was soulful, it was black love, old loves, it was the latest dances

I remember when music was empowering to our people Marvin said, "Brother, Brother, Brother there are far too many of you dying, we've got to find a way to bring some love in here today"
Today it's Twirk that monkey, if you don't give a d••• go on throw it up and I need a freak and we all know
I need a freak to let me stick it down her throat

It was say it loud, "I'm black and I'm proud"
As we degrade our beauty and define it by how much T. N. A. we can show and how low we can go to the flo' make our knees touch our elbows-I wonder just how low we can really go
Music was a chant that led our people to freedom
It was a drum beat that communicated to our fellow tribesmen
It was story time, a griot and storytelling
Now our legs propped open soliciting the second class status we once fought against…now we're fighting, begging for degradation by bragging about killing, pimping and stealing

As I lay in bed at night I wonder if our brothers and sisters have any clue of our power, potential, our history, our struggle, our love, our justice, our blackness, our beauty, our historical existence in this universe
Do we have any clue as to our true existence, talent and strength?
Do we know about the struggles of Sojourner, Fredrick, Mary, Martin and Malcolm

Now instead of shooting for the stars we are shooting at one another
Do we care about the struggles of the masters of the pen-Langston, Sonia, Nikki?

You see I remember when our music was our voice for social change
A deeper experience, a tool for a cultural exchange
And I know back in that little ol' town called Ville Plate
A strong black man had to tip his hat
For fear that it would be a sign of disrespect
and that was the equivalent of a lynching, no laws to protect
Him or Us

Music was that chant that Big Momma sang in the fields that led slaves to freedom
It was empowerment
It was our form of communication

And now where are we?

Crimes on Childhood

His childhood was stolen
A.I.D.S had kidnapped his parents
Trespassed into his youth
Robbed him of his childhood
Denied him a simple tuck in bed
No I love yous or good nights said
Burglarized tomorrows

Committed battery on his adulthood because his youth is on life support close to death
and adulthood is on a respirator just a matter of time before the decision will be made to
pull the plug
cause who cares about the dark continent

As he bribes life for just a dream rather than his usual nightmare
Blackmails the ghost of his ancestors for a storybook ending, his tucks in bed become a
molestation of life

A conspiracy to hide his future within a land field of excuses and red tape
No life saving meds before it's too late

Jacked of feeling loved
Prayers to God above
Lord breathe life here
Memories held hostage by a death demon
As the semen of horror deprives him of hot meals

The death demon deprives him of life
The death demon commits crimes on his childhood

The Wedding

There's a wedding today
There's a wedding today

She's 8 years old and today she's leaving her mother and father, sisters and brothers, dolls and jump rope, swing and laughter

She will live with her future in-laws until they decide that her temple is ready for entering

The temple many times not fully structured
The temple topples; it receives a permanent paralysis because too much has entered it

Her dowry released her to them but now her body releases the fluids of degradation, the stench of pain, the foul odor of primitive traditions which could kill her because her temple now leaks uncontrollably as her childhood falls out of her into a pail of embarrassment that she holds beneath her

She may walk miles to reach a bus that might take her to a hospital but if passengers find life's stench to be unbearable, yet cultures tradition of implementations stench a must, for her they say leave
Leave hopes destination
Go away to die
Go away to become permanently deformed
Paralyzed with life's harsh reality

There's a wedding today
There's a wedding today

She's eight years old
Her story rarely told

Her soul sold
Through dowry's tradition
Destructive conditions
Life's ambitions- Crushed

There's a wedding today

Two Thousand Five

We are the proud, the few, the disenfranchised
And like Maya says, "Still We Rise"
Our voices a glass seal atop
Left in impoverished ghettos like fruit with rot
Stolen elections
And no protection for those who attempt to do right
Unreadable votes
Young brothers and sisters stand up take note
Now after 9/11 and no link to Sadaam or Alkida
Dieing mothers and fathers, dieing jet fighters

Sending our families in to rebuild
When even armed soldiers are still targets for their kill

What's the plan in a foreign land
that we invaded?

What's the idea for foreign soil?
A brothers in jail for stealing a pack of cigarettes but what about that oil?

Dark seeds of the motherland
It's time; It's time to take a stand
Make a change, rearrange and be all that we can be
Influence world thought because they do see

They know who we are
But do we know who we are?

A. I. D. S

They were in love
Maybe she more than he but love none the less

He was good until he drank
Red Bull, Budweiser, Old English she had to thank

He had let the drugs go, long ago but too late to avoid the fate of a diseased blood stream
some say from running women, some from the down low but who knows where it really
came from
All we cared about was the outcome

In a massive secretion exchange
After he married her he'd made little or no change
Yet
They'd made 4 beautiful girls
They'd made 4 beautiful black pearls

Killed that mother with the secretions of
A. I. D. S.
Left them here for a grandmother to raise
And to that grandmother I give much praise

He murdered my childhood friend
Left embarrassment and family members to pretend
What happened? Said she had cancer but the real answer was buried deep beneath the
beautiful image of her journey

She'd passed away from the painful pricks of a scornful needle that infected her pride and
kept her there with him in grim circumstances

Chocolate Child

As a child there were moments when I wished for straighter hair and a lighter skin tone
You know those moments when the commercial describes beautiful healthy hair as silky
and shiny and the model would swing her head around and her hair would move with the
wind…at that moment I'd curse my heritage and my ancestor's kinks
You know those moments when adults complimented only the light skinned children on
their looks and over looked the Black Pearl in the group
The teacher that let only the mulatto looking students run her errands, spoke softer
to, had more patience for and bragged to the other teachers about how beautiful those
children were
Today this chocolate is my trophy
It's my reward from the Lord
And people who keep wanting to tear me down are those who wish they were me because
their reality is that with no substance, no class and lack of drive
In this world whether light or dark you won't thrive
Sometimes that crutch weakens your strive
Because you think the worlds gonna' do for you just because you're alive
And you have lighter skin

You had nothing I wanted

It was the way you intentionally made me feel
It was the self worth that had not yet been instilled
It was your ability to peel away my value and further drill into me that I was not as good
as you

Society seems to have seen you as beautiful because of your "good" hair and light skin and
you embraced the status with full force
Media and family my only resource
For knowledge
What hard work had you done to make your hair naturally straight rather than course?
What personal sacrifices had you made to earn the self proclaimed higher status of lighter
skin?
What made chocolate covered candy the sin?
Flaunting that others would remember you for your beauty but not me the invisible
shadow that lurked beneath you
Well what were they going to remember me for?
Oh, that's right they didn't notice me
They were blinded and couldn't see,
the Black Pearl in the group
Just how hard did you have to work to get that light color?
Now you're having a breakdown because you've discovered that it hadn't propelled you
anywhere

I was accused of having problems with God's shades of greatness
Some of those shades of greatness are having the problem because this true to life Nubian
Queen is in her season
My upward movements propelled by God himself
I make no apology for it
All that darkness created an inner core of greatness and now I stand before you
Loving me
Completely, whole healthy and happy

Find Yourself

Devastation

The earth shook and our children died.

Planes dived into the lives of thousands and we wept.

The wind blew and our grandmothers were left abandoned under withering heat.

A wave arose and our mothers disappeared.

The fires ran through the wilderness and our sisters and brothers lost their way, burned and perished.

Dreams turned to smoky clouds of grief.

The sides of mountains eroded and our laughter was shifted into the cracks of infinite mourning.

Some say it's a sign of Revelations

Some say it's man's abuse of the earth

Some say God is angry
Angry that we are living immoral lives
Angry that we ignore his presence
Angry
But hasn't there always been those who defy God?
Haven't we always had sinners almost from the very beginning?
Have our sins grown worse?
Are we mocking God now?
Is this why?

B••••, Trick, H••

*This poem was written to bring about awareness of the extreme negative images of African American women that presently plague some art forms. It is meant to provoke thought and to encourage change.

I was the leader of African dynasties
And now I'm your tip drill
And like the Tin Man and the Scarecrow I lack a heart or a brain

All the same
I love you

I once was the mother that held your seed, gave life to the extension of you
And now I'm your Chicken head
The only position for me in your company is my body propped on a bed

All the same
I'm here for you

I used to be the one you came to for comfort when your heart was shattered, when your body was bruised I helped you to heal after the floggings but today I'm anybodies slut
And we don't cut for each other anymore

All the same
I'm standing by you

At one time we stood together, weathered all storms
We loved each other without conditions
Now I'm your b••••

I once was Big Momma cooking, cleaning, advising, protecting , directing
And now I'm a skeezer
Reduced to a naked teaser in a video better known as "Video H••"

I stood by you through the marches, dogs, water hoses, sit ins and now I'm a walking c•••
And yea I'm blunt
because this is our reality

As we become pawns in a pimp game of
whatever sells

Big money goes to big boss man and some money goes to us
Well G what's the fuss?

The fuss is that surprisingly sisters the darkness that shadows our truth is not new

What's new is the visual reinforcements
A neatly packaged group of gyrating black tramps soaring around the world and propping one definition

of who we are in the world's face as they chase the pot of gold that isn't at the end of the rainbow

What's new is the lack of boundaries and regard we have for one another
The lack of keeping the sanctity of our sisters and brothers

I was the one you loved and protected
Now rejected and neglected
You were the one I'd cared for through life's crisis
We'd carry each other on the backs of our father's values and our mother's determination
And now our ancestors cry WHY? What happened?

Well you say what's the big deal
The big deal is AIDS
We all get played
A lack of respect for our gifts and worst our lives
The destruction of our relationships- no husbands with wives
History is rewritten to create facades of nothingness

Entire generations are being raised on satanic images that suggest that the beauty in their walk and the creativity in their talk
Is limited to one thing- their bodies

Our children catch hell because they lack value in our eyes
And I refuse to make excuses anymore
I'm not anybody's wh•••
I'm your sister, your daughter, your mother and your grandmother

I'm your best friend
That sister that cuts for you until the very end

I was Big Momma, the leader of African dynasties, carried your seeds
Met your needs
And I still love you

Is the Bank of Justice Bankrupt?

Does It Have Insufficient Funds?

Can we cash the check of justice here in America?
A check where upon demand the riches of freedom and the security of justice will be given to us
In God We Trust
Can we trust that our children and our children's children will receive justice?

Equal education doesn't mean equal pay
We all know less pay means less say

Is the Bank of Justice Bankrupt?
Does it have insufficient funds?

An overwhelming number of African-Americans are still living in poverty compared to whites
And we don't see the plight
Because at night
when we turn on our TVs we see bling, bling
Oprah giving away cars and J. Z. doing his thing
But
Our criminal justice system over sentences young black seeds
There is a need
To revamp
We are overdrawn

Has the bright day of justice emerged?

Now is the time to rise from the dark and desolate valleys of segregation to the sunlit path of racial justice

Majority of our schools are selectively segregated today
The ancestors believed in our education, they dug the pathway
And they prefer to transfer their funds to make a way
For their own

Again and again we must rise to the majestic heights of meeting physical force with soul force
Of course we can't overlook violence against one another
Scrounging for the crumbs left on ghetto's tables and dumpsters
And our youngsters
Don't see that their freedom isn't free

Has justice rolled down like waters and righteousness like a mighty stream?
Well it seems that way

When will we be satisfied?
When there are no more police beatings
In a long song of not guilty, mentally emotionally defeating

When racial profiling is a thing of the past
Then We Can Truly Cry Free at Last

Food For Thought

As skeletons approach
Hearts sank
There is no help for this mother
It was just too late
Too late to feed her shadow
He died atop of mounting graves
She walks away to bury the seed she bore
Almost emotionless cause skeletons walk lonely paths all around her table
No, "Let us thank Him for the food"
There was none
Infants gasp lifeless whispering cries of hunger "Feed me, Feed me"

Tummies ballooned to infinity
While victims play wait and see, wait and see if we will be…wait
WAIT
Cause help is a comin', help is a comin'

While thousands wilt from the evaporation of the world's cares
How much can this mother bare?

Her baby didn't make it
Strapped to her back as though he still feels
She leaves to give him back to the earth
Not imagining that when she gave birth
he'd leave her this way

But help is a comin', help is a comin'

Not soon enough to save her son
Not soon enough to save this precious little one

Their eyes cry tears of hopelessness and there is no rest from this drought brought about
by the burning heat seemingly from Lucifer's fire because only he could cultivate such
destruction
Only he could conspire to kill this baby
Save me! Save me!

I just need to eat
Can I cheat death and live?

I just need to eat
Can the drumbeat of my heart continue to play the sweet melodies of life?

I just need to eat

As skeletons approach, hearts sink
And we think
While death's brink
creates endless darkness for her

Rwanda

There were 80,000 dead and America barely blinked
80,000 dead and America barely blinked
80,000 dead and America barely blinked

As tears from red eyes flow down dirt roads like red veins
Hurt, heartache, pain slide down dark cheeks and their blinks become darkness for lives
lost as survivors try to rebuild burned spirits

Visions of heartless torture and empty tomorrows,
Buries their happiness in infinite sorrows

Our lids closed to the pleas and cries of mothers losing their children, listening to their
entire families slaughtered
That..... had replaced free, loving, yesterdays

And salt water drops into wounds as the world looks the other way and their children
don't play anymore

We don't even care enough to issue Viseen to make it look better, to patch the massacre of
the babies, children, mothers, fathers, grandparents

The veins of weeping eyes paint pictures of lines of bloody bodies along the streets
And we sleep
While our brothers and sisters die
Their loved ones cry
Kneel before the sky to ask God why?

Rows of dead bodies align the streets
As survivors weep
Cowards retreat
Raped until he got tired
Under the lens of diseased

minds
Setting their lives afire

There were 80,000 dead and America barely blinked

Reparations

I'm all for reparations
But how much do you owe me for erasing my family name?
Auctioned off naked bodies, how much to rid the shame?

How much should you pay me for each lynching, burning, beating?
How much for the theft of my life and then cowardly retreating?

How do you pay me back for the uprooting of my family tree?
I'm all for reparations but what quantity for what was done to me?

This country was built upon the backs of my ancestors-crops, herds, housing, carpentry,
inventions... their intention, to keep me poor and uneducated
While we waited
For freedom that wasn't free
I'm all for reparations for what was done to me

How much do you owe me for the deliberate denial of my education?
Separations from mothers, husbands, first born
Left to mourn the loss of a future

What amount for each rape?
How much for each limb?
When I attempted my escapes

What's the cost for the child sold from her mother?
How much do they owe me?
How much to recover?

For the chained, packed, filth they cargoed us through
For painting our American dreams black and blue

How much do you owe me?
Nearly any amount would be an insult, a slap in the face
For we are the backbones, that's right my race

So when they offer up their amount
Remember to calculate thoroughly cause everything counts

Embezzled Birthdays

He died before he could get his first shave.

He was just eleven and on his way to heaven.

Cause life had been sketched on an abstract pad limiting his purpose.

Growing up too fast
Like a closed top, the streets turned up the heat and when his ambitions rose he couldn't knock the lid off,
So mothers in black dresses and big hats form lines to mourn the death of wilted visions.

Rows of future black kings trying to look hard, sit and can't openly admit that inside, their hearts beat faster than President Bush's lie detector needle.

Don't we know yet that those who slay their own youth are doomed to parish?
But my son, yes I did cherish.

This poem was suppose to be about the life of my son.

The one who always hugged away my tears, said the right things at the right time.

This poem was suppose to be about his first facial hair, his growth, little league games

But

Premature coffins spread across foggy fields of dishonesty.
We lie, we deny, our mothers cry as we let the streets define him.
I saw him practicing how to be hard and

I said nothing.

The gates to his future locked as I allowed him to flounder in the dirt and manure left from societies antonyms, portraying who he was.

I want to tell all the brothers I know how this movies gonna end
'cause in this script mothers don't send their babies off to college they send them off to coffins when we don't explain.....
Ill-gotten treasures are of no value but righteousness delivers from death.

We betray them
We betray them by not taking them under our wings and later we sing funeral songs like, "May the Works I've Done"

So for all the stolen birthdays
I say let's catch the thief and put him away
and give our sons back that special day
More birthdays as presents, a manhood for gifts and allow him to become the blessing.

Katrina

The leadership said he couldn't honor the request
Because the important paperwork hadn't crossed his desk

While we watched our TV and felt their pleas
As our people, after 4 days began to drop to their knees

Overwhelmed with desires to help cause I knew more could be done
For these the true children of the rising sun

Our nations president laid in his hammock in Crawford, Texas drinking cold lemonade
soaking up the fun

He won the election, said we were safer today
Yet our people were dieing needlessly while listening to him say
"The leader of FEMA is doing a heck of a job"
Anybody with a heart sat in front of their TVs and sobbed

As the tears of a grandchild fell from that little ones face

The world watched Nannie lose life's race

See that was Big Mamma, Cousin Rae Rae and Aunt Pookie
It was an umbilical cord connection to us and a subhuman touch to others cause they look
like our family

Nowhere to sleep, No food to eat
In a country overflowing with milk and honey

Save yourselves sisters and brothers
Get a plan for your children, cousins and mothers
Cause they don't care about us
After 4 days public leaders didn't receive papers for the request of a bus

We've got to rescue the colorful foundation of America on our own
The fabric of this nation right here was sewn

Our preachers support leaders that flew over dying dark faces,
 that wilted and withered needlessly

Sleeping outside in dangerous dark places

The richest country in the world could not save our babies

The boojie blacks who've forgotten where they came from support leaders who lie there is no tie to 9/11
2,000 dead 3,000 in heaven

His policies can only be described as faith based bribes
Still lapping behind him knowing he's lied

And the war in Iraq is not based on fact
As they stack the bodies one on top of the other and their mothers can't even get a meeting

Over a mournful mother's tears
And a child's fears, they'll never see mommy again

Safer today?
We weren't prepared for Katrina and she told us she was on her way

Yet I can still hear our leader say "The leader of FEMA is doing a heck of a job"

Her Death Row

She waits for them to burn her flesh.

She was a baby making babies ....
While the church ladies.....disowned her

Her children never knew her, not really
See she was locked up before they knew what life was, before they took their first steps,
before they could explore the depths of her knowledge

The sins committed were against God's law and human beings have no forgiveness
They'll be there to witness ....to witness the burning of her flesh

Families wait months for one conversation, one word, one more look into each others
eyes
during evening skies
And sorrowful goodbyes

She'll never see freedom
Her dreams are dead, decaying
Just like the bodies of the people she killed and her death date is the ultimate delaying

She waits for her death, the burning of her soul

While under the states control-her and her children's future

She'll sit in a seat that will take her....
to her maker
A seat that will not deplete the grief that she's caused

Her wishes for her seed are different from other mothers cause just to attend
their games, see them off to school, wash their clothes, assist them with brushing their
teeth, advise them through a rough adolescence is beyond reach
she attempts to teach
Behind bars
But she'll never be able to erase the scars she's left

The bars keep her from a hug, a kiss
She reflects on all the growth spurts she's missed
Appeals and wills
Wills and appeals
They write
Victims fight

Emotions take flight and all we can see is a murderer
She's a battered mother
She's an abused daughter

She waits for them to burn her flesh

A Trick's Product

I'm the product of a trick
Don't get me wrong, I love my mother
very much but I am the product of a trick

She got hooked to a pipe filled with
white rocky escapes, floated into a land
of hard luck hazes and cemetery dazes,
hallucinogenic crazes

She walked the dark streets at night
searching for comfort
She found a gang rape....so here I am

It's not her fault cause in this society it's
O.K. to sell the pipe
Festered with drugs
Satan nips and tugs
Taking pieces of her with him

Tortured her existence
Lowered her resistance
Ain't nothing wrong with a little hit now
and again
But those hits became her end

While carrying me... she got lost at sea
and how I came to be
I was the product of a trick
He controlled her soul

When I was born my mother was doing
time, 6 to 9

I was fortunate I got to be born clean
And my mother, well she's still my queen
I didn't miss out on the love of a family
or anything

Growing up the question, who is my dad
brought about anger
So I just went into an imaginary photo
album and chose my dad from books that
told secrets of past lives

Her life was rough
Her living too tough
for a caramel rose in the mist of weeds
that created a foggy route of values and
morals

I'm the product of a trick and a true
success story
See I am my uncles only son and I'm also
his pride and glory
He stepped in and took over
He held me high upon his shoulders
And yes, I am the product of a trick

The Boot

Stolen spirits
Tears
Heartache
Death's dance around young playful souls
Fearful fathers protect what they can hold
Young brothers take on patrol
Heartless higher ups remain out of touch
And asking for the basics was just too
much
Washed away dreams
Through poverty's theme
Sunkin' lives
Lights out
The Boot showed us what our lives were
really about
Dark nights on dark faces…
Horrors in common places
Washed away futures
Pieced together dreams
"You did it, no it's your fault!" their
political theme
The ruthlessness of it all

Pointing fingers and blame games persist
While heartless legends serve in our mist

Souls stuck in attics with the ghost of our
ancestral injustices

Hunger
Misplaced
Helping hands
Lewding or surviving which one?
Crimes or survival techniques?
Criminals or survivors?

Instead of sending food and water, they
sent the National Guard to protect the
'haves' stuff
They knew that what they already had
wasn't enough

How can our leaders be so out of touch?

Deaths dance around young playful souls
Fearful fathers protect what they can
hold
While young brothers take patrol

A New Address

Three young faces look up and want to know through whistling winds that blow where's mommy?
They'd lived through drunken hazes of begging and pleading
They'd surfed through the sounds of their mothers body tossed against what was suppose to be a sanctuary- their home
They'd pray at night that mom was alright but one day mom wasn't alright
There was a certain silence that day
Three young faces woke up from where they lay
A silence like no other morning
But it wasn't like those 3 little faces hadn't had warning
Even though they were young they understood pain
And on that silent morning their sunshine became a life long rain
Because on that final morning mom was no more
God had come to get her and take her sole, her core
Now she lives with him
She had no intentions of ever leaving them
There are three little faces that miss there mom's touch
Three little faces that needed her very much
There are three little faces that look for her at night
And through their little faces we feel her visions, her sight
Fractures of her life took over her body and he was to blame
She'll be missed dearly and loved just the same
There are three little faces who hurt tonight
Three little faces that will one day see some light
Because God's going to guide those three little faces to a grand success
And I knew their mother she was full of zest
Just knowing her throughout childhood I've been wondrously blessed
She's in one of many mansions now she has a new address

HOT CHOCOLATE

Love poems

Love Me

"Let's let's stay together, loving you
whether, whether times are good, bad,
happy or sad, Let's, let's stay together"
Al Greene

We can weather this

Was it the drug infestation in our
community that shredded our spirits in
the 70's and 80's
Ladies do we condemn him when he
strives to please us?
Cause we lack trust

Men do you overlook her fineness
Take for granted her kindness
Then treat her like less than the queen
that she actually is

When slavery's ugly journey took us to
the unknown darkness of wives and
daughters raped in front of their
men..."We stayed together"
We loved….We nurtured….We
weathered

When our men were forced to breed with
others to produce new inventory
"We stayed together"
Lived to tell the story, the story of
unconditional love

There are many ways to castrate a black
man
But we took the stand that, "We'd stay
together"

Many ways to destroy the spiritual
wealth of a black woman but we'd work
through it

Our brothers bare the stench of racism
far more than we will ever know

We must push forward to grow
And show "We can stay together"

Young brothers kicked out of school for
minor offenses
Charged with felonies so they can't get
jobs or vote
So I devote this poem to my brothers and
to the lovers who remain committed to
this love thang

You see baby I know I bring baggage
and so do you
But I'm willing to be that train that pulls
 you through

What did my momma teach me?
Why was my daddy gone?
Is this why we can't relate? Why we
can't get along?
Baby, tonight like Marvin Gaye says
"Let's get it on"
Cause tonight I'm singing this song cause
I want to stay together
I just need you to be the structure that
supports me through this thang

We need to cooperate and not dominate
because only 48% of our families are
headed by married couples

Our unmanaged conflict leads to
frustration
We need to show more appreciation
While frustration leads to disengagement
Then hard times spent
Disengagement is a sure route to
infidelity
So just tell me what you want from me
Instead of what you don't want

I'll share my wishes with you baby if
you'll share your dreams with me
I am that hole and you are my key
to staying together

Provocative Planet

I dream of the cloistered moments
I long for the sweaty seductive seconds
I crave the galvanized hours of unrestricted affection
I yearn for the days of undying devotion
I hunger for the weltering weeks of wet wants
I thirst for the mammoned months of amorous love making
I require devoted years of yes's
I desire decades of "I dos"
Let's set fire to the seductive centuries of our very own sexual love scene
Let's become one on our own private provocative planet

My Chocolate Covered Dream

Chocolate
Chiseled
Spicy
Soul
Hard
Sexy

He is a chocolate covered dream
Ladies you know what I mean- Fine
A strong sexy thing
An African King

Perfectly carved and chiseled to
perfection
And his affection
is just a monument placed on the
 historical grounds of my soul

He is sexy and every hard curve on his
 body is a chocolate mound of satisfaction
An overt reaction
A chemical attraction

Full lips that softly sup my conscience

That beautiful brother
Who's sensitive to the needs of his
mother

He is a chocolate covered dream
written into my own poetic love scene
And with everything
he'd make my flower sing
He is my everything

He IS love to me
Because at just a brief glance I could see
all that our love was going to be

My thoughts become sunshine through
rainy days
Just his soothing voice calms my waves

He is a chocolate covered dream
written into my poetic love scene

I want him in my world forever
Leaving him- never
Because
He is like no other and today
I stand before God and all to say

We'll love one another forever

Support each other through every
endeavor

And all I ever want to do is
completely and totally love you

Y'all he is fine
He is so fine

He is smooth like warm chocolate
He is just so fine

My heart sinks at the thought of his
presence in my universe

You know what I'm talking about ladies

He's that brother that has enlisted in your
Love Army

He's that private that salutes you just
upon mere thought
He's that lieutenant that stands at
attention
At the mention of your name

Chocolate
Chiseled
Spicy
Soul
Hard
Sexy

My Chocolate Covered Dream

Poetic Flick

Instructions: Take 2 excitement pills every 4 hours with poetic play. Don't exceed 4 levels of excitement within 24 hours.

Warning: Not to be heard by individuals with small minds. Exceeding more than 30 minutes of poetic flicks could result in sudden jealousy.

Imagine this my favorite poet and myself will enter our candlelit bedroom

I'll lay on a bed of poetic panteums and my favorite poet will kneel over me before entering the elevated ideas of my emotions

There will be rhythmic sounds simultaneously as we reach our first socially conscience climax

I read my poetic partners lines
And hypnotically he reads mine

We co-instantaneously know which scene we want to place our viewers into next

Together we produce lyrics that cause your mate to float into our sestinas of fantasies

Tell me are you turned on?
Am I pimping you?
Am I being pimped?

These words are just that, words so don't hate the poet. Take 2 excitement pills every 4 hours with poetic play and if jealously persist for more than 2 days contact your local relationship counselor.

Taken correctly will result in extended lovemaking with your partner

Not to be taken with jealous boyfriends, girlfriends, husbands or wives. May cause sudden side affects such as hostility, hard hearts in men and quivering legs in women

Not to be taken with any other poetic inhibiters

This has been a public service announcement

Frozen Moments

I just wanted to freeze the moment
That moment when you looked into my
eyes, said nothing but told me how much
you loved me in the glance

I just wanted to freeze the moment when
our poetry intertwined and became
beautiful perspirations of bountiful
desires

I wanted to freeze that moment and hold
you near forever

But I couldn't

You blew into my insane world and made
it seem sane if only for the moment
I grasp that moment and allow it to fester
it's sweet fragrance into my diary of
unspoken love and that way I really
won't ever have to let you go

I wish I could freeze the moment when I
realized you were writing me into your
poetry the same way I wrote you into
mine

When our lyrical lips met
When we made love through poetic
verses
Letting go was impossible so I just want
to freeze the moment

SOLID CHOCOLATE

Poetry, prose and short stories for and about men

Brothers I Love You

(dedicated to the late Oliniyi Labinjo who inspired this piece)

To all the brothers who take responsibility and who nurture their seeds
To all the brothers who care for someone else's mouths to feed
To all the brothers who protect their Black Queens
To all the brothers who've written us into their love scenes
To all the brothers who make a serious effort to care for their families
Who stand up for righteousness in the face of a Babylonian world
Made us the center of their cinnamon swirls

To all the brothers who cringe when I'm disrespected
To every brother's spirit of whom we've connected

For all the times you've shot that extra dose of self-confidence in me when I was too
afraid to get on this mic
For all the times you said "G that was tight"

For all the times you've opened a door, changed a flat
Gave me a compliment when I was feeling fat

Picked me up after someone else knocked me down
Inspired my writing from your own creative, melodic sounds

Gave me a hug when my heart was heavy

Came to my rescue when I couldn't get my car started
Gave me that extra glance and winked when we parted

Loved me inspite of my bloated, moody, monthly moments
Forgave me when I wasn't on it

Brothers for all that I love you
STAY STRONG

He

Every time she looked at him she saw the reason why her life ended

He looked just like him
So she beat him unmercifully for everything and even for nothing

An absent father left a weed to grow wild and be nurtured by the elements

For some reason he took more than his younger brother
Even though they were of the same cloth
that cloth that smothered his stability

Perhaps he had been the unexpected seed that tarnished her reputation and forced her
into a marriage formulated in Hell's Sanctuary

Perhaps she'd not been nurtured herself
Maybe no one had ever held her without a motive

When he couldn't defend himself
When he couldn't defend his mother through her own storms inflicted by a weathering
demon called dad
And it's so sad that all we see is a homeless, useless cracked out brother because mother
was unaccepting
It was her way
Her lay
And her play
Her fault
Her choice
And his voice was a silent one planted deep inside the womb of her existence

Too mean to see the full scheme of things
And blinded by the mirror of truths, unable to look herself in the face
Because she would always go to a little place in her mind
that describes her child rearing time
as shameful and wasted

All she knew was that Revelations had come; her virgin like image was gone
Replaced with the moans of a labored motherhood

No anesthetic for neighborhood gossip
She was the latest topic of conversation at the local coffee house and every time that pain came
When other mothers would have cut some slack
It ended up on his back

Having survived the beatings of his mother, and the rejection of his father
He's still capable of loving

Sure he's messed up
He can't keep a job, he sleeps in his car, he tells wild stories
Maybe those stories come from the world he'd wished he'd lived in;
concocted from childhood fantasies in places he'd been when he couldn't bare reality anymore
And he might be your eyesore
The bunt of your jokes
But he be my kin folk

Oh, he's just crazy
No he's a survivor
And dope was his way to cope
Still he exist capable of loving
Capable of nurturing and still a man

Where Are My Brothers?

At birth mother coddled and protected
But society's rules he's still subjected
Later society's values rejected
His ability to feel has been affected

At childhood momma defended
Momma accused them
They're picking on him
Prejudice and stereotypes is where their
bias stemmed
They're using lies to condemn

MY SON

In his adolescence mother let behaviors
slide, boys will be boys
When do you encourage him to put
down his toys
Didn't you know being soft destroys?

MY FUTURE HUSBAND

As he enters his adulthood his values are
clouded ....He hadn't been taught
Throughout his life momma fought
Now doesn't do what a good daddy
ought

Where is my husband, my daddy, my
brother?

Is he taking his last breath?
Is he cracked out close to death?
Is he pimping women right and left

Mothers wake up and rescue your sons
by challenging them to be great
Stop waking up when it's too late
And mold him into a good mate

FOR ME

Did You Tell Her?

Did you tell her she wasn't good enough for you while you were inside her dreams?

Did you tell her she wasn't cute enough for you while she cooked your meals, pouring all her love into each recipe for your future?

Did she know she wasn't pretty enough while she took you around, introduced you to your aspirations and helped you grow, did she know?

Did you show her that you didn't love
her while penetrating her security?
Did she know that everything about you lacked masculine maturity?

Was she not good enough when she
chauffeured you to your jobs,
appointments, and parties because you
were incapable of maneuvering your own future?

Did you tell her she wasn't good enough
while she put her dreams in a box, placed
it deep into a treasure chest of potential,
just to help you fulfill yours?
Allowed your weaknesses to seep into

her pores,
And resurface as ugly little blotches on her reputation.

When your pockets were empty she gave
you love offerings but she is just a thing
to be used, emotionally abused.

Mirror, Mirror on the wall whose the
fairest of them all?
Your mirror lied to you.

She wasn't pretty enough for you, your
mirror told you, you were beautiful
enough to lie, mistreat, then retreat

Your mirror lied to you.

Truth be told you aren't good enough for
her.
Hell, we've been mistakenly calling you
sir, when it should've been ma'am.

You wouldn't have survived without her kindness, her strength, her pockets.

She reached deep inside herself to help
you survive, to keep you alive and in
return, you didn't tell her!

Where Were You When.......

Where were you?
Where were you when those older boys chased me from the bus stop with rocks while
calling me mono negro

Where were you?
Where were you when the pipes burst and worst
where were you when the first boy I dated broke my heart?
Why have you distanced yourself?
Why are we so far apart?

Where were you when the Asian convenient store clerk
Called me a little black nigger and pushed me out of his store
at age four?
Why have I been ignored?

Why have I been left so unprotected?
Why am I feeling so rejected?
Has my birth really left your life unaffected?

Is it your poor daily choices?
Are your new women and their voices
whispering jealousies fire into your heart?
Is this why we're apart?

Why have you vanished in the fog of my yesterdays and storms of my tomorrows?
Why?
You see I no longer cry,

The warmth of God's spirit has comforted me but I need you, you are the only one who
holds the position of dad in my world
I was your bundle of joy, your very special girl

Now I'm scorned for being strong
but I've been without you for so long
Considered wrong for having to do it on my own

So yes I push you out of the way when you want to help me with a bag
I call someone else for help if I just can't do it myself

I become a safire when you have a demand
Because I've always had to stand
Alone

I don't expect you to open the door because at its core it hurts if I expect and you don't
So I just won't allow it

So forgive me as I work through this pain
Forgive me while I go through this meltdown
I'm just not used to your unconditional kindness but
I do want to love you
So I won't ask where you were again.
I'll ask where will you be
I'm praying here for you and for me

Where will you be?

To the Undercover Brothers

She was the dark and lovely
cover girl and he, a queer
eye for a straight lie

She is the wrap of warmth
A beautiful hanging display
She is a well stitched work
of art
Her quality strong and first
rate
Her patterns are radiant,
auspicious, alluring
Unaware of the danger he
places her in
Unaware of his secret late
night sins
No indications of where he's
been
Didn't know her entire
marriage was his
opportunity to pretend
She thought she was the
love of his life
She thought she'd been cast
in a leading role as the wife
but she was just an extra
She was the cover for a
brother who was on stage
She was an overcast , his
security
She was the bedding that
masked his homosexuality,
his self-truths, his denials

She was the huge lie
displayed for the public, the
artwork in the window of
the "Down-Low Brother's
Store"

Tearing up a future
Ripping down a past
Snagging the present
and
Stinking up lives

Discoloring her beauty with
the heat of his sexual
passions for a man Too
weak to take a stand and
just be the man that leaves
her out of it

Storylines riddled with male
sex toys and female's joys

It feels better, more
courageous, stronger to say

I'm not really gay

but I can play her husband
on the stage of life

Act out his role fully as a
 husband should to a wife

But too selfish to be real
with her or his own life

No, he feels better
discoloring her beauty,
tearing up futures, ripping
down past, snagging the
present and stinking up lives

You see patches of a life
ain't it just pieces of a future
until perfectly stitched to
make a beautiful cover

Daddy Seal

Her child, a small fish in a circus called
"Manipulate the Family"
Come One!
Come All and see father seal perform
amazing fetes!
As spectators enter and take their seats
To see a well rehearsed show of
misconceptions
The seal trainer comes out, "O.K. father
seal you must turn flips, do dips, don't
move your lips and finally you better not
trip or else you won't get the treat- You
won't you see your daughter"
The whole show is a calculated
performance of illusions
Jump through this hoop and maybe I'll....
Do a flip and maybe I'll ....
Jump off a diving board, oh not high
enough, can't see your daughter this
month
Single daddy seal out
He doesn't fully know what the games
about
Toss the ball of hurt and manipulation to
the rest of the seal family for each of
them it's a balancing act of don't piss the
trainer off
The seal trainer is a wonderful actress
very amusing, very animated and very
believable

An expert in the field of illusions
You see, the audience doesn't see the
misuse of the seals so the final conclusion
is that the audience sees a show
Father seal misses an opportunity to see
his off springs grow
Father seal sinks below
Sea level
His insides wither because he loves his
baby but it's always maybe
Maybe tomorrow

Maybe next week
Maybe
Maybe next month
Maybe next year
Maybe
Her child is a small fish in a show called
Manipulate the Family

Reverend

He lurked in the prayer rooms and in the
small offices of the church
Like a vulture up high he'd sit right there perched

He drove up in a broke down, faded
powder blue Pinto
He was big and towering, thus I looked
up to him
He wore a long, dark robe with a
colorful cloak around his neck suggesting
power, a clean spirit and holiness
At the time who was to think any less
Touching little boys in dark corners..
comforting at funerals words of
encouragement for families and other
mourners
The audacity of him to misuse his power
The audacity of him to pervert our Lock-
Ins during late night hours
Laying more than his hands on souls
Pretending to rid them of Satanic strong
holds
Assuring that these seeds will never grow
old
enough to see a middle aged tomorrow
 ....today he is cocky and bold

Instead of praying for us he was preying
on us
The flock let their sons spend nights with
him, go on camping trips alone
Now at age 17 Johnny discovers AIDS
full blown
Parents trusted him, he had a wife the
highly visible Sister Cover Up
Because within his own bed the boys
he'd tuck

Violating the most precious of temples..
our children .... our little boys
Manufactured them into his own private
sex toys

A healthy view of manhood and a sense
of self Rev. destroyed

He ruthlessly shatters their dreams,
tarnishes self images, digs scars into
souls that will never heal …Their future
this preacher peeled away and left them

scared, confused, broken
No one would've believed them if they'd
spoken
And sure enough when the flock found
out, to the world's surprise
They preferred to obscure Rev's lifestyle
and his lies
Worshipping the man and not the Lord
while he pries open their son's thighs
He drenches their adolescence with
lubricated perceptions about who they
were yet to become
They were game pieces in a Satanic
ritual only he calls fun
Rev you see is a self proclaimed "Oral
Freak"
Within the congregation little boys he
seeks

We're not talking about a minor
indiscretion
We're talking about a lifetime of
deception
A holiness perception

I'm speaking for the scared little boys
who once were my friends and who now
cry out from their graves- He's not a
man of God! He's not a man of God!
He's not a man of God!

As the boys withered their way into
young men Rev gave them a facade of
humanity right there on the grounds of
the church
Where upon high he still sits perched

And admired... kept him from hell's
fire... But nothing will save him from
hates desire

He'd created the cries, the ghost of dead
young men begging for life

He now drives a fully loaded Mercedes
His members cannot see the danger in
What their futures may come to be ... You
See I grew up in that community!
He has the charisma of a David Coresh,
The power of Jim Jones and that petrifies
me

Dying to Worship

Veronica Reddon was just 14, not very attractive and probably experiencing the same plights most other 14 year old adolescent girls were experiencing. Her communication with her parents had broken down due her need for independence and her parent's need to protect her. Then there was tremendous pressure to smoke and have sex not just from peers but society in general. Veronica constantly felt awkward and left out of most social settings. Teenagers don't usually opt to go to church when having problems. So what she was about to do was completely out of character. She decided to go to church. That's right she went to church, Cal Baptist Church around the corner. She had heard that there was a young, new preacher there, and while she went with negative expectations; she was pleasantly surprised.

A young, slightly overweight pleasant man walked slowly to the podium. He wasn't dressed like a minister, and he wasn't married. After his sermon, she thought to herself, he didn't condemn her in his message."Hi, I'm Reverend Dr. Frank Fielder" and Veronica thought, man this church is different. He spoke of forgiveness and laying your burdens on the altar and leaving them there. He had a wonderful sense of humor. She laughed that night, something she hadn't done in a very long time. God had spoken to her and she knew it. While still sitting on the bright, cushioned red pew seats she had a feeling that all of her problems were being left inside the church that night and everything was on its way to being alright.

The community where the church was located was also the community where Veronica had grown up. Attendance had dropped at the church in the past several years but they had heard about this wonderful new minister and were eager to hear what he had to say. They fell in love with him right away. This was just what this community needed. This was a predominantly upper-middle class community, known for its manicured lawns and high profiled people and having a minister who obtained his Ph.D. in theology in their church was just the right fit for them, most of them were educated business people. The young people adored him because he was still rather young and playful, making him relatable to them. He was a win, win kind of a brother. Most everyone in the community knew each other because they'd lived there for years, raised their families there and had begun to raise their grandchildren there.

Reverend Fielder's sermons were a refreshing, change from the traditional services she had gone to with her grandmother when she was a little girl. As the church grew rapidly the pastor formed many youth organizations and this really saved Veronica's life. She had been hanging out with the wrong crowd and now she didn't have time for them anymore, she was learning how to live a holy life through one of the many organizations implemented by the pastor. And there were just as many organizations for the young men of the church to help them through life also. The youth went to camp, took over night trips, performed and occasionally spent the night in the church. It was great! The church took care of most of the expenses so everyone could participate especially the youth that didn't have the means.

The church had grown so rapidly that soon it was necessary to build a larger facility that would hold everyone. When the new facility was built it was massive and beautiful and it still felt like home. The people were still connected to one another, but as time went on Veronica noticed that Reverend Fielder never spoke of any form of sexual immorality. She never brought it up because some of the youth counselors spoke about sex in the Bible studies they would have but she thought it was odd that he didn't say anything against fornication. Didn't most pastors denounce premarital sex, homosexuality, adultery, bestiality and any other forms of sexual sins? Maybe those subjects were too sensitive. She noticed that he had begun to speak less frequently. She noticed that he wasn't at church very often. But, she wasn't alarmed because there were many wonderful associate pastors there who took his place, besides he was probably spreading the gospel at other churches, traveling and helping others. When he did come back she noticed he had become more flamboyant. He wore loud colors and once told the congregation that he had spent $1,500 on the sweater that he was wearing. His sermons changed too. He told more jokes, used profanity, often skipped using scriptures and repeatedly boasted about the money he was spending. He had also become arrogant, daring them to express any dissatisfaction with his behavior. Still, the congregation was proud that they had such a fabulous, jet setting minister. They were most accepting of his behavior, which amazed Veronica.

One Sunday, he announced his engagement to a woman who magically arrived and had never been seen before by anyone in the congregation or by those close to him. Reverend Fielder was born in Flagstaff, North Dakota. He had lived there through his teenage years and then he moved to Dallas,

Texas to attend college. He isn't from this area maybe she's one of his "home girls", that's why we had not seen or heard of her prior to this moment. We don't have to know everything about him; again Veronica explains her suspicions away. It seemed as though he was friendlier to persons with status; maybe it was because they were able to help him develop the new wing of the church or could donate more goods to the church bazaar.

It had been rumored that the Reverend Dr. Fielder had been accused of sexual harassment at an all male university where he had been a professor of theology, but nothing could be proven so the university just asked him to resign and he did. He then applied for pastoral duties at Missionary Baptist where he began pastoring. Rumors started to fly, none of which were believable. One high school boy, Peter, a member of the church and very popular at the local high school, accused the pastor of trying to kiss him and fondling his genital area. He told his parents and to his surprise, they didn't want the issue addressed, especially in public. It was more embarrassing to make this public than it would be to just pretend it never happened so why would he tell anyone, he could gain nothing but humiliation by exposing the beloved pastor. It was more important for Peter's parents to keep their status in the community. Besides Reverend Fielder had helped them build their contracting business, how could they possibly betray him by exposing his dirty little pass time? Veronica felt a sense of terror run down her entire body. She had grown up with Peter and knew he wouldn't lie about a thing like this. It soon became apparent to Veronica that the pastor was most friendly to the families with young sons. He liked little boys. Still like many she stayed, even as other young men started to come forward she stayed.

One bright sunny Sunday, Veronica arrived at church as she always did; she entered the side sanctuary doors and found her favorite pew. She always sat third row center on the end. The organ started to play, a scripture was read, the choir began to sing loudly and harmoniously. The holy spirit filled the room, when suddenly a young man wearing a lavender tie shirt, fitted white pants and processed hair stood up and yelled out, "Reverend Fielder I don't know why you fronting, don't act like you don't know!" The choir stopped, the musicians froze like mannequins in a department store window. The entire congregation became silent all eyes and ears were on the colorful character standing in the center isle of the church. Reverend Fielder seemed unmoved by this odd display, obviously meant to embarrass him. He said calmly, "Sir, I will speak with you later". . The ushers quickly escorted the man out the back doors of the church and even that wild, unexplained escapade didn't alarm the congregation. No one asked questions! They did whisper amongst themselves and soon the fire from that died down, too.

The Christians who had a sincere interest in growing in their faith had begun to look for other houses of worship by this point but still Reverend Fielder had a huge following and thousands of supporters in spite of all that had transpired but many had stopped going to church altogether some becoming former believers. When Veronica came home from her after school job she turned on the 10 o'clock local news, put her belongings down on the sofa, as she did every night, but this day proved to be very different. She got a quick flash of what was going to be coming up after the commercial, the news commentator stated local minister makes disturbing statements. She had a feeling that it was her pastor, even though it could have been anyone, something told her it was and sure enough it was him.

One of his lovers had tape-recorded a conversation of Reverend Fielder explaining that he "loved licking little boys and the little boys loved to lick him". The secretly taped conversation gave indications that Reverend Fielder was in an establishment asking for young male strippers and paying for their services. In the coming weeks the media continued to press the pastor for a response. He pandered to the public by using buzz words such as Homophobic, clouding the real issues and knowing that these words would bring various advocates out to fight on his behalf, he continued manipulating the media but the members of the church who found his behavior alarming were unwavering and so was he. He made it seem as though the church members had a special hatred for all homosexuals and lesbians, knowing that the real issue was his untruths. He vowed never to leave.

Veronica was sick to her stomach. Her mind started flashing like a movie camera on rewind. She began to think of all the nights she spent in that church, who was sick and dying now, who did the pastor seem to like the most, how could she have missed that? What was she thinking? How blind could they all be? The unusually high number of members on the church board who had died of AIDS should have been some indication. Then she began to realize that the other adults knew, they had to have known about his controversial past, they hired him. They had to have known that the university that had previously employed him had some ethical questions concerning his behavior with his students. Surely they had gotten references from his previous employers and even if the school didn't release the details of his sorted past, Sister Vionna and Sister Carlson surely would have found out. They could get any information at any time anywhere. These two sisters knew everything about this community and if they didn't know, it didn't happen. Certainly the adults at the church didn't expose their own children to this man and then continue to expose them after they knew he was a threat to their safety. Surely, they would have done everything they could to protect their own children after they discovered the pastors dirty little secrets. Well they didn't; making excuses to remain in that house of 'worship'. As Veronica reflected on how far she had come spiritually and her overall experience with Reverend Fielder and Cal Baptist Church she realized that she had grown to know God. She felt that she had met the Lord right there at Cal. She felt that Reverend Fielder still had some great qualities but she was not willing to sacrifice her salvation for that. She was not "dying to worship".

MOCHA LACE

Poetry and prose for women

Wh•••

She's a wh••• stay away from her
We heard it time and time again while
we were growing up

Have you had sex before …wh•••….wh•••…..wh•••?

How long did it last? Did you ask for…… more….more….more?

How many sex partners have you had at
once? …..four…..four ……four

Well, doesn't everybody keep score…score…..score?

She was really a soldier fighting on a
battlefield, in her mind winning the war
It was one more battle she'd won
She had been in this fight a long time

Fought by enemies who ruthlessly
entered her
Broke her down psychologically,
Numbed her,
Tortured her spirit,
Forced her to keep THEIR dirty little
secrets

Because the secret code was always a
hole dug deep beneath the surface of
truth, where she would be placed but not
him
Where the bowls of other soldiers were
discarded
She became the thing, less than a real
woman but still a woman

In this fight the enemy is rarely seen as
spoiled, damaged goods, he's just a man
with a plan

Going about a daily activity while her
tears flow the cum of his fowl march

And we as women look at her with
judgmental stares
This issue divides our glares
Because we see the end results
Bambi the sex worker and Sexual
Chocolate the porn queen

The only training needed for these
positions was their ability to go numb
because for some
It was the only way to survive

She's not a victim, she's a wh•••
Be on the man's side, revile her even
more

Waving our Bibles and condemning her
to hell
Because sex sells
And we buy
We'll hurl the word at her, hitting her
with it
Bruising, breaking
Bending, shaking
As pimps and johns start over taking
Making Wh•••

You see immediately she's tried and
convicted not the perpetrator
And no witnesses come forward because
they hide beneath the blankets of
embarrassment and shame
But all the same
She's "hoeing around"

The victim then becomes the town slut
And we cut for the perpetrator
"Men will be men", "That's a man for
ya' "

In a 4 year old's gleam, she lost her
shine
He's tarnished her with the smears of
ejaculated perversions and she now
becomes less than a woman, while he
remains more than a man

Midnight Sisters

Holding our heads high embracing their validations because of
imitations...historical credit for our
creations

I remember when these lips were called
Soup Coolers and exaggerated in comic
strips and made fun of by family
members and friends
Those same family members and friends
now embrace after collagen infected
homemade beauty was shot into invisible
lines referred to as lips
Now painful expensive butt implants to
look like these hips
I remember the Twin Peaks jokes, that
referred to my well endowed, God given blessings
Unsolicited pokes and degradation
chokes, Itty Biddy Tiddy Committee Membership Card revoked
Breast implants leaking envies poison
through self hates blood stream
Playing make believe in a
psychologically, murderous Hollywood
scene
I remember being too black to be
beautiful
Hair too nappy, not that good stuff

Joke filled smirks and dimwitted stares,
from darkness Seeds of the Motherland
glares, childhood burdens to bare,
Prayers to God "Oh God Please Give Me
Good Hair"
But if God made the all the hair, he
didn't make any mistakes
Slapping on lubricated lye to erase any
trace of the African race

I wished I had known then what I know
now that I am black and beautiful and
black is beautiful
And that the hate that immersed itself in
my life was really envy of who

I naturally am
I am midnight black
I am nappy
I am colorful
I am creative
I am rhythm
I am rhyme
I am unique
A saucy satirist who will speak…truths
I am deep
I am a treat
It's only natural for them to want to
compete
With this Nubian Goddess, that's me

Daughter

Tiny pieces of future fell from me in flesh colored droplets
Portions of destiny floated in a tub of pain
As parts of tomorrows became yesterday's regrets
Fragments of hope, were scraped from my womb
And the world, become a cold instrument of destruction
I had just begun to rearrange emotional shelves and she'd have had everything because I
had made a place for her in the windows of my soul, hung old behaviors in a closet of
contentment just to make parts for new beginnings
And there was nothing I could do
There will be no birthdays, no first steps, no feelings of pride a mother feels
There will be no dance recitals, no piano lessons, no ribbons and bows, no lacy dresses
No please moms and reluctant yeses
She fell from me in the form of flesh colored droplets
So there will be no sunflowers dancing in the recital of a mother's gleam of sheer
perfections
No bedtime melodys from the piano keys of my heart
Because my precious baby girl and I were forced to part
The strains and stresses of everyday
No opportunities to mold her like clay
My baby girl had passed away

Tiny pieces of future fell from me in flesh colored droplets

Timeworn Women

Lord please don't allow me to become
them

Drowning in yesterday's sorrows
Visions of darkness in my every tomorrow
Clothes of happiness desires to borrow

Tied to the bitterness of last year's wrongs
Singing every old heart ache, pain and love song
Inviting manipulation and his cousin control along

Living alone and vicariously through others
Mean and missions of dreams to smother
Searching for history's lies to uncover

Heavy hearted with burdens of yesterday's stings
The stench of loathing their presence brings

"Nobody Wants You When You're Down and Out" blues songs they sing

Laced with jealousies of successes of others
Blankets of failure their mission to cover
Desires of destruction damaging another

Broken, irreparable, useless to the world
Insults, havoc, fruitlessness hurled
Hurting, slandering, complacent all swirled

I want my smile to be the world's sunshine an aura to bring the seed of those who come in
contact with me to full bloom with just a kind word or a simple phrase

Hearts lightened through mitigations praise
Thankful to God for my many days
Complete turns from wicked ways

Road Trip

He touched her
She knew it was wrong
He calculatingly used mental manipulation so she'd play along

He knew it was perverted but it felt so good,
How would others react to her if she exposed his sick desire for her?
It started with a fun tickle, an innocent touch
Progressed into a ride proven too much

She was only 11 and he her 35 year old stepfather
Well, he had all planned like he was mapping out a road trip
Became her buddy then into her he'd slip

He sadistically planned his route to penetrate her sole, to wreck her innocence
It started with a tickle and ended with a trickle
Plowing through her
Not realizing that his sick desire for her was creating a future drug addict because drugs numb
For some

Said she was teasing him with her tight jeans and cut off shirts
Teasing him with her cute mini skirts
He'd come in drunk and slipped into her bedroom to violently consume her

Mother was sick and dying of cancer
Why was her daughter on drugs and walking the streets at night?
Her predator had all the answers

Momma called her fast,
switching around here and showing your past

It's probably that little boy down the street
Look like you talk to everyone of them you meet

You know my man didn't touch you girl, you done made that up
Always seeking attention not to mention,
Now you're spoiled, damaged goods
Who would want you now?
Take a bow for all that acting you're doing

So most of us just keep it inside allowing it to poison our destiny
You see it's time to be free

98

It was nothing you've done
He touched you when your adolescence had barely begun

Healing is in order and forgiveness, the first step
Through all tragedies our Lord God has kept

Remember you are valuable

Beneath a Midnight Sky

Beneath a midnight sky I saw it
A Nubian flower alone tattered by life's winds
Walking on a dark road and as I approached I realized that it was a Nubian Goddess
carrying the seed of life, A new generation
And even under that dark night sky I could see she was sick
Body decaying from the poison of the earth
A man made pesticide meant to wither her beauty and it had

I wondered why she was on this dark journey alone
Does she need help?
As she approached I realized that she had a destination
It was a van of Satan's Angels willing to accept whatever she was willing to put out for
whatever they were willing to give her

I know this because they didn't look anything like her
I wanted so desperately to help my sister even if it was just an encouraging word but I sat
there paralyzed with my own fears
Wondering what would her van load of Johns do, what would she do?

I pulled up along side after she got in the van
Hoping to inflict some sort of embarrassing snapshot of them
Something that would engrain in them that what they were about to do was so utterly
harmful, disgusting, incredibly sad

A thief had come in the night and stolen life from what once was a queen in her
own right

Her life reduced to the defecations of a suicidal society

Famine

I used to think it was just a slight oversight
You know, the undernourishment of our bodies for the past
A self imposed fast
Sometimes openly insulted and trashed

I believed we weren't teaching our children the history in our schools because it was so
close to all that testing ...You know that determines whether your child is smart enough
to go to the next grade
Although in every aspect of our lives Black History was made
But not one textbook nor curriculum nor test is that history conveyed

I honestly felt that since that portion of history wasn't on the test that this was our reason
for the starvation of knowledge
I didn't discover that there was more to me until I went away to college
We wouldn't have separate African-American studies if our textbooks would've
acknowledged
So attempts to destroy a separate program would leave the history completely abolished

Then one day we fed the hungry ... the food of enlightenment ...The masses became
petrified
There would really be no need to do it if the curriculum included our side
You're putting our history down they cried
Let's promote European History they sighed

I honestly thought the masses wanted to be fed... I thought they had a desire to drink
of the Liquid Spirit of Edification ....Longed for more education ....desired intellectual
elevation

The masses perceived the giving of knowledge as an attempt to under feed them
Martin Luther King and slavery were the portions we skimmed
One black history program left us fed but still trim

It saddened me so that I wrote this poem in an effort to say; if one gets fed and another is
already being fed
Accept the blessings of equality

ASSORTED SWEETS

Families
Poetry, prose and short stories

Lonely Child

He beat her in her face, turned it black and blue
He told her he got another pregnant, so that she already knew

He called her names and belittled her yet she chose to stay
It was only when his child needed him did she threaten to go away

She's only eight but already in their eyes, too late to salvage
Too late to be nurtured into a better being,
freeing themselves from the burden of this young life
because his wife had a problem with it
She just doesn't fit into her agenda

The grandmother said, "Let the witch go into foster care"
She was beaten and blamed for the problems that were already there

Her mother's mother sexually molested her
So her mother didn't know how to mother her

The cycle then recycles
The cycle then recycles
The cycle then recycles

She's eight and takes mood pills
So she rearranges those feels

Those hurtful touches
Those hateful insults
Those threatening stares
You see foster care, was best for her

But isn't it ashamed that she has grandmothers?

A daddy, who sadly, openly says, "I don't love you", "I don't want you" , "I'm through caring for you"

Isn't it ashamed that today we've lost sight of the values our ancestors gave
We are more educated and yet we're still enslaved

Enslaved to a system we rely on to rear our children when we don't feel like it
And yet too proud to admit
The selfishness within
Snooty attitudes and uppity vibes
Yet unable to care for our own as we describe
How many material things we've acquired
And yet too tired for the inconvenience of our own children

The cycle then recycles
The cycle then recycles
The cycle then recycles

What will happen to her now?
What will she become?
Will they come running with excuses when they see her success?
Will they try to claim her when society recognizes her quests?
Will they ask for money, share in her fame when she shines as best?
Best at succeeding in life inspite of them
Best at shining a light on the dark and grim
Best at overcoming

Best at breaking the cycle

Half Sisters

There's one man two mothers
There's two daughters and one father
Which equals hurt, pain, anger, shame

Half sisters joined by one
Separated by some.

Half sisters reaching arms stretched to each other pulled a part by Satan's frustrations.

Always a feeble attempt to make us compete for attention from family members full of
pretenders
Who compare us as though we are sports competitors.
Entangled in deceptions barriers and it's ashamed we've had to be pulled apart this way,
but sister one day we'll make our own decisions for our lives.

A love like no other,
A love that can't be smothered
By deceitful mothers hiding under lies
covers.

Angry at a father whose always been there for both.

Angry at a father whose never had much but was willing to give that of which he did have.

Raised apart, left to sort through recycled lies
A clouded, spurned mothers late night cries.

Unanswered questions of why daddy isn't here to tuck me in
Was my birth his curse, my sin?
Momma says you come over and pretend.

Just being my daddy was your sin.

But daddy I see you, I love you and you do what you can for me.

We'll come together,
Life's umbilical cords tied unsevered.

Same blood running through our veins
Angry mothers full of blame
Pointing fingers their claim to fame
Images of each all tarnished and stained
He's where he is and where he's going to be nothing lost,
Nothing gained.

But it doesn't have to be this way
If adults would act like adults
Cast their own feelings aside
Swallow some of that pinned up pride
Let some things slide
And just let us be sisters.

Family Reunion

Sweet Big Momma calling wrong names
"You know who I'm calling boy, ya'll all look the same"

Nice Aunt Sarah got the sweet potato pies
Soothing sweet sounds of babies cries

Cousin June Bug smoking the best barbecue
Great Aunt Mae stirring that Louisiana roux

Little ones running, hollering, knocking things over
Fussing and crying then laying on shoulders

Man how you've grown
This is my baby Sig
Man, last time I saw you, you were this big

Playing cards and talking smack
but you ain't worried
Somebody at the table always has your back

Buzzed Uncle Bill talking loud and telling jokes
Done poured his spirits in his can of Coke

And Old Uncle Willie with the big pimp hat
The Huggie Bear suit and the 70's Cadillac

Reminiscing, hey remember when......
It ain't nothing like visiting your kin
Cause ain't nothing like hanging with good folks

Sitting around laugh, eating good
food and telling jokes

A beautiful festival of love
and interesting rides

A carnival of colorful personalities

And an amusement part of adoration

Cherished puzzle pieces fitting perfectly
as we open the pages of our family
history through the eyes of our elders

Walking the bright path of past ages
Cherished new beginnings as seeds
blossom to carry the bloodline on

That's a family reunion

The Ring

He began his day before the sun rose and ended it when it went down

Deprived of an education yet thrived,
strived and kept his family alive
High moral character for him meant blessings

Blessed in spite of
Blessed because of

Seven seeds nurtured
Straight and narrow

In spite of, he gave, he gave

His family had more than they needed and some of the wants

Two graduating at the same time
He worked even harder to get the rings seemed like a simple thing
but his daughters were finishing high school
A simple gold circle with antique linings, embracing a large H
The H meant
Hard work
Heart
High moral character
Higher roads

But to a destructive force it meant nothing

The long hours
The sweat
The determination
It meant nothing

One blow and the ring would go
Crushed dreams, dashed hopes, tarnished memories

One blow
Thank God he was already in heaven
He didn't know
Of the destruction

The ring….seems like such a mundane thing
but
It was hard work
It was achievement
It was morality in spite of
It was the ultimate symbol of love
It was God's grace from heaven above

It was the ultimate sacrifice
It was his faith in Jesus Christ
One blow and the ring would go
Crushed dreams, dashed hopes, tarnished memories

Beautiful Skin of Ebony

How is it that her spirit was so sweet?
Her persona was aromatic and savory, permeating everyone she'd greet
Her beloved presence in everyone she touches was a true, sincere treat
The matriarch of this family, God gave us the best to complete

Where did her angelic sense of humor come from?
Her presence was my warmth, my morning sun
As she'd grown wiser she never lost her knack for fun
We bear witness to this through hearts she'd won

When did she develop her astounding sensitivity?
Could it be that her sensitivity
Provided me
With the superb example of who I needed to be?
She mirrored for me
How to get on my knees
And thank Thee
For all that he has done for me

She held that get up and go spirit
I pray that I will have that same heavenly wit
When she walked into the room the atmosphere was lit

When she dressed, everything matched
Her shoes, matched the dress, that matched the purse that matched the hat
Everybody knew Mrs. Deshotel when upon the pew she sat

Chose quality merchandise
Appreciated all things nice
One day I'll be able to use her shopping

advice
And purchase those things that are very nice

And yes she was particular about her possessions
But her wisdom advice to us- Don't put those things over our affections
God first, family next is the Deshotel sequential connection

Her warmth comes from the sun
Her experiences with God stitched souls together as she sat at her sewing machine and spun
Grandmother, you are all of what I will become

What makes you love the Lord so much?
You encouraged us to lean on him as our crutch
You've instilled within that everything's O.K. with God's divine touch

She kept so very busy
I thirst for that unique fervor inside me
As I observed her tend her garden inside that beautiful skin of ebony

From the simple calls she made each day
To the common things she used to say

All come back as crystal clear mountainous memories
The love she'd give can't be replaced
The woven emotions cling to my skin like finely stitched lace

Why was she so loved in her community?
Because everyone sees what I see
It was my beautiful loving grandmother inside that soft, beautiful skin of ebony

Dys-funk-tion

At about 1. a.m. the family was awakened by glass crashing! One thunderous crash after another. Frightened it was an unwelcomed intruder each family member grabbed a household item for use as a weapon. Slowly one after the other they crept down the hallway when they realized that Laila, the youngest daughter wasn't with them. Oh my God! Was the intruder holding her hostage? Was he assaulting her? Hearts were pounding. Bessie, Laila's mother recounts how she thought she was having a heart attack. "My heart was pounding so hard and fast it hurt." They all stopped just before they reached the kitchen when big brother Earl got in front and jolted himself into the kitchen area where the noise was coming from, hoping to startle the criminal who had boldly entered their home and was probably planning to kill them all! To everyone's amazement Laila stood their pulling plates from the cabinet one by one smashing them onto the white linoleum tile floor, yelling "I'm tired of y'all whispering about me, you ain't nothing either!" Her impulsive, fragmented statements and violent outburst weren't new to her family. Bessie's fright turned immediately to her notorious enabling manner. "Well she's just upset", says Bessie, "She thought y'all said something about her". Her sisters Althea and Annette become angry but say nothing. It's 1. a.m. in the morning, we were dreaming, who would be discussing her right now? But they knew that saying anything would make them the culprits and her even more so a victim. It would be like throwing a lit match on a stack of explosives. Laila becomes more agitated and even more violent when trying to calm her. Her behavior was often unprovoked, sporadic and totally unexplainable.

Brother Earl takes a different approach. "Girl, stop throwing those plates! You need help it's something wrong with you!" He always could get away with saying more than the girls could. Laila looked at him as though she was in a daze and began threatening him using every 4-letter word she knew. This is when the situation becomes most dangerous because Earl can "crank up" and get violent too; he just had more control over his behavior than Laila. "Now y'all let's just calm down and Earl you leave Laila alone you ain't perfect yourself!" says Bessie as she grabs a broom to begin to clean the small ceramic fragments that once were her plates and now represents the lives of her children from the floor. Rather than tangle himself in the transparent dysfunction of his own family he chooses to pack a small overnight bag and go to a friend's place for the night. Althea and Annette feel an urge to do the same but as always they are torn between helping their mother with Laila, (Laila could have another outburst and hurt their mom) and living normal happy lives, separate of this dysfunctional triangle.

The following day Althea and Annette meet at Captain John's a local seafood restaurant to discuss their family situation. They both agree that there is a problem but disagree on how to deal with it.

Annette begins, "Girl, I'm sick of this; I just want to move out of town somewhere!"

Althea, "I think we should schedule an intervention."

"What? An intervention! What is that, some type of psycho mumbo jumbo?", Althea seemed agitated.

"I saw this on a talk show where the family members and closest friends have a meeting with the person who has a problem, they tell the person with the problem how their behavior is affecting their life, as well as, the people and situations around them, then they tell them how they have to change or they aren't going to deal with them anymore."

Annette, "Please! Do you really think momma and Laila are going to agree with that bull crap?" This has gone on for so long and the suggestions of getting Laila help in the past have always gone ignored. You know momma is more embarrassed of her getting the help she really needs than she is of the things Laila does!"

Althea, "You're right about that but I think we're going to have to do something. We can't just keep ignoring it. I'm scared she's going to hurt somebody or herself, if that happens I don't know if I could live with the guilt I'd feel, especially if she hurts momma."

Annette, "Again I think we should just leave. Neither momma nor Laila have hit bottom yet. She hasn't gone through enough with Laila, so when we say something, anything, in an effort to help her, she turns on us. I say we move to another state, let them have at it, and if momma ever feels she's had enough she'll try to get some help. Look at all the things we've gone through already. Remember that time she wanted mom's car keys so she screamed in her face, backed her into a corner and was yelling, give me the keys bitch, and less than 10 minutes later she asked calmly for the keys and momma gave them to her. We tried to intervene then and momma wouldn't admit that there was something wrong".

Althea, "Yea, and I remember that incident when her boyfriend had to call the police because she became angry about something, and broke all the windows out of his apartment and his car. Do you remember that? "

Annette, "Yes I do, she was angry because he ordered pizza and she wanted hamburgers.", the sisters laugh trying to find some humor in this obvious mirage of painful reminiscing. "And remember when she left me on the side of the road late one night because she had forgotten to turn the headlights on on the car and I reminded her. Oh my God! She was yelling and screaming you ain't nothing, f- you. Girl, it was crazy that night. I had to walk to a pay phone to call you to come get me."

Althea, "Yea, I remember."

Annette, "That night mom asked me what had I done to her to make her treat me that way, girl, I felt all alone at that moment, standing on the side of a dark freeway, unsure of my exact location because I had never been there before having to walk to a pay phone, then standing next to a strange man who had come up. Momma accused me of doing something to Laila to make her leave me there. It was a mess! Let's just leave the state, this is the only way we can have a life. Let me say it again, if momma ever feels she's had enough she'll seek some help."

Althea, "Laila broke that broche Grandmother Nan gave momma. That broche had been in the family for many generations."

Annette, "She didn't just break it she destroyed it. Grandmother Nan had cleaned houses day and night and worked extra odd jobs to buy that broche, it meant so much to her, I remember Laila wanted to put it on a chain to wear around her neck. It didn't bother her at all how hurt momma was about the whole thing. She literally destroyed the broche. I was going to take it to a jeweler and see if he could restore it as close to its original design as possible but momma had thrown it away already. Again I say let's just leave town and let them have at it, they'll finally get enough and seek help".

"I don't know about that," Althea rebuttals in a defeating voice, "Both of them need counseling. I also know you can't force anyone into treatment."

As Althea and Annette leave the restaurant they bump into sister Laila. "Hey, I wish I had known you were coming, we could've met. Her cheerful demeanor and pleasant disposition was classic. Her personality was like a pendulum swinging back and forth only this pendulum was totally unpredictable. Althea and Annette explained that they had already eaten, and that they were headed home to rest. "Oh please! I'll treat, have coffee and desert with me", pleaded Laila. The girls thought about it and agreed, it's rare that Laila was pleasant and this could be the perfect opportunity to encourage her to seek help for her sporadic, violent episodes. The sisters started with pleasant conversations. When Laila was like this she could be so much fun. She told jokes and they laughed out loud. They asked Laila about starting a business because Laila had a Ph.D. in Business Finance and she was most willing to share her knowledge. While she appeared to be in a state of "normal" as Althea and Annette preferred to think of it, they decided to address the issue of Laila seeking professional help.

Althea begins the dialogue, "You know Laila.......Uhm, the other night," she pauses then musters up the courage to continue, "You frightened us, throwing those dishes".

Annette adds, "Yea, girl and it was just crazy, we were frightened almost to death. We thought someone had broken into the house".

Althea tries to soften the advice that she wants to give to her sister, "You know we love you but we are afraid of you and we want you to get help. We think you may be Bipolar".

"I agree with Althea, you really may need some medication", Annette adds.

The reaction Althea and Annette got shocked them. Laila's eyes began to well up with tears. "You're afraid of me?" she asked in a soft tone. The girls looked at each other, wasn't that her intent, to frighten them? She really does need professional help the girls thought. Laila verbally agreed that maybe she does need help, but in her mind she had no intentions of getting any, deep down inside she felt that she was normal and that the world had the problems. Her reactions to everyday situations in her mind were the problems of others and they need to adjust not her.

The sisters left the restaurant still unsettled about the future, accepting the fact that nobody can force a family member to get help, they have to seek it on their own and if they're not made to feel that there's anything wrong with what they've done then their isn't any motivation to get better.

Lines

(inspired by visual artist Lisa Kristine)

Every line in her face is a journey towards knowledge

A pathway to wisdom
A tunnel of love
An indention of care
Hard work and legends told

Those lines are roads walked long and lonely

The warmth of her garments are felt by all

Tiny pebbles of poverty roll rampantly through the streets
While cracks in walls tell secret stories of yesterday

Her garments are the endless galaxies of legends told around campfires

Her brown skin bares the weathering of her existence
And those lines in her face are the stories told of the ancestors

They lead us to the heavens

Respected and valued for her wisdom

There's beauty in those lines

She is the journey towards knowledge
A pathway to wisdom
Tunnels of love
Indentions of care

CHOCOLATE SHAVINGS

Relationships
Poetry, prose and short stories

Mad Mondays

It feels so bad ya'll

My blue Sundays rolled into mad Mondays
He'd turned his back on me

It feels so bad ya'll

You see he had been my late night special
My come when I call him
My everything, he made my flower sing
With everything he'd brought laughter

One day he decided he wasn't really in love

And it felt so bad ya'll

I ached, I thought I'd never stop hurting
I thought we'd always be flirting in endless tomorrows
In our old age, how was I to gage where we'd end up?

We'd spent our days making love
You know the kind of love that included holding my hand..... just being my man
Just listening to me... you see he was everything to me

Thought I'd never want another
He was love to me

But he was an actor and I his prop
While he pretended to be something he was not

I give and I give and I give
I feel myself becoming a self-loving anorexic

I feed his ego and in return I get little nibblets of crud, "a baby I love you here" and "you
are so special to me there"

But never enough to feed me, never enough
I hold on to the disease to please

While praying that he consumes a daily dose of vitamin C to see me as the queen that I am
The vitamin D that detoxifies the nature within his soul that destroys

As I go on with my existence it gets better and I know he longs for what he lost

But it feels so bad, it feels so bad

I was the best of everything that he had ever had

Totaled

Driving down that highway of love
Got the top down on the old used Corvette enjoying the sky above

Got distracted and hit a bump or did the bump hit me
You see he and I had a few scratches and dents none too noticeable to see
Never felt a need to fix or repair them it was sufficient to let it be

But when that car hit something or something hit me
My engine felt pain because the wreck included three
Love Insurance was my company

My fate was out of my control
Love Insurance had to respond with fixin' it or totaling my soul

Love Insurance sent Unsure Tow Truck to pull it into the repair shop

Here my heart was to heal at this paltry little stop

I'm here to get a new paint job, to get new shining wheels
To replace my crushed chrome heart
So once again I can feel

Love Insurance declared my heart was totaled out
Here comes a big new car note rest assured without a doubt

But all isn't lost because a new car always smells good
And at least in the beginning, it always does what it should

My new car reminds me that I can get through it when I never thought I could
Right there from beginning to end there by my side the Lord stood

Where Are My Love Poems?

Where are my love poems?

My love is in those rocky mountains of lies, cheats, deceits and hiking retreats

There in a sea of desires, burning uncontrolled forest fires, winding trails of professional liars

My love poems, My love poems
Are in the Louisiana Swamps being eaten by parasites, manifested in lonely nights,
Desirous of unseen sights

They fester in bayous of left over waste, trusting romantic gestures often misplaced,
heart wondering in areas poison ivy laced

Lost in a storm of dark clouds, thunder, lightening, tornadoes, and unforgettable floods
Trapped me on a path of sliding mud, washed away all loves flower buds

It's been thrown in the recycle bin used and reused, defective products I chose, eroding
trust you lose

You were sat out by the curve with the other trash picked up by someone who thought
it looked good, like a proud piece of trash there you stood, I'd stamp a manufacturer's
warning label on you if I could

My love has been chewed up and digested and flushed away, my desire was to have you
stay, why does your tree stomp lead you astray?

Where are my love poems?

My love poems have been stomped on through the ritualistic dances of those who practice
littering all over town, sewers filled with deceits beat down, covering the beauty of
nature's ground
                              AND
THERE THERE is where my love poems are found

Not Really Love

When love becomes a permanent cessation of all vital functions
The end of feelings

The passing or destruction of something intimate

When love causes injury or damage
A blow
A wound on your heart

When your lover is the killer of your belief in true intimacy

When the reality of love is actually decayed, spoiled, foul, tainted and sour

Hate becomes the result of a deliberate
hit from your significant other

And all that you've ever known is that love was supposed to be honest
               honorable
               sincere and
               whole-hearted

Can someone tell me how to balance the reality of what is with how it should be?

Should I see love as a satanic game where declarations that are not true
               fraudulence
               inaccuracies and
               falsifications
make you a winner in the game of love?

What is the prize in the game of love when your strategies were
               falsehoods
               misrepresentations
               misstatements?

A contaminated conglomerate of mess

That really isn't love at all

True Loves Avenue

The feeling is actually gone this time
I remember when it was unimaginable
that you wouldn't be mine
You, You were my favorite headline
You were my ultimate sunshine
My chocolate covered oh so fine

I no longer want to hit pause-rewind just to hear your potent voice soothing me through
Comforting loving words from your mouth you spew
I still love you but I also grew
It's easier now....True love.....I'm due

I no longer see you as the strong
protector I had come to know
Our sunshine and rain created this
beautiful incandescent rainbow
but through hurting me your weaknesses
show

I've loved you with my whole heart only
to have you throw it back at me
You've crushed it, ground it up into
small pieces like grains of sand
Marrying me...was that really your
ultimate plan?

It was a culmination, results of a
transformation of a tainted image of you
There's courage here now
Your indiscretions I won't allow

It's too late
What you had you didn't appreciate
I guess this was meant to be our fate

It's too late
How many times was I suppose to let you back only to suck the life from my subsequent
being

I saw you with her it plays over and over again it's all I keep seeing
It's too late

I'm obviously not the woman you need me to be
It took this long for me to see
Because true love doesn't include three
Baby, you were more than enough me

You can't hang onto me while you continue to look
No more of my self-esteem at one point you took
Dropping me emotions shook
Stealing all my insides like a common crook

I can't cry over you anymore
I can't try with you anymore
I won't even ask why anymore

It's been 3 months since you've phoned
Emotionally I've moved on
No more of maybes love prolonged

I've said it before again and again
trying to convince myself
All the while emotions put away on my "Secret Loves and Passions Shelf"

My heart was actually dedicated to you
You mistreated it, mishandled, minimized, misused and maligned it and now I've started
anew
It's now strolling on "True Loves Avenue"

House of Higher Ground

When his heating and cooling system changes at the flip of a switch
When any tail wags makes him twitch
When those romantic lines are mechanical and sound like a pimps pitch.....And you know it
Then crying to your girls about how he's a dog and ain't worth a bit
YOU let him taste the sweetness of your lips
Because you're sure he's going to commit to you and your body or at least he's going to lose his mind for it

Closets where dreams are left hanging
While time goes by and our sizes change
Styles change and minds play games
Targets take aim and we struggle for claims
Masking the pain

Walls of hidden lies that we tell ourselves
When we know our desire is to have a good man
A strong structure to stand
A rock and a wedding band

Get that mirror to see yourself
Know that laying everywhere affects your health
Could block and destroy your wealth
Cabinets of hidden secrets and desires
Stoves of unlit sexual fires

Cooking up dishes of perpetual liars

Allowing your breast
To be the pillows upon which Mr. Unworthy finds his rest
Makes demands instead of requests
Where your home continues to settle for less

You're cooking meals, offering your bed

Then sending him home to his wife and his other girlfriend
Talking about you don't want him anyway
He's just something to do right now
You could win an Academy Award with those words so take a bow
He gives you all the dust and dirt you allow

Don't cast your pearls to swine
While you are in your "anything goes" state of mind
With the word is where you need to align
Because there's someone worthy to bask in your sunshine
Well a sister got needs
And I understand that but don't sell yourself short because a brother got needs too
Open your window and see another view
Higher floors you've got to pursue
Otherwise you become just another rusty, used screw

Why?

Why won't I let you love me?
Because when I've let you inside me to see my naked vulnerability
You became my scrutiny
You were the decoy and I the prey

I've let you in time and time again and you've been my self-hate
Once jocking me hard now staying out late

So I'm severing my ties with the creepers and the cheaters
And the self-esteem beaters

You've loved me today and have not been IN love within my yet to come hopeless
tomorrows
Finding pleasure as I trickled down soggy paths of sorrows

Left me broken, fractured my yesterdays
While I was down you taunted me, developing these distrusting pathways

Took your pencil and erased my future because my future was you and you alone
Why won't I let you love me?

No, I don't want to love anymore and I don't want anyone to love me
Liars and predators....their infiltration is what I see

Don't feel sorrow
For this is not a sorrowful poem

Maybe my harsh todays will turn into softer tomorrows but today it's sunny
Players, your antics I find funny

Who you are with, what you're lying

about today or even where you were last night.....
I ain't trippin', ain't gonna be no fight

Cause I ain't grippen'
false realities
Ain't slippen' into the trap of "caught up"
I'm dealing with self-truths, life's truths

Oh you choose me now, why?
Why now?
I show you no interest and so what happens when I let you catch me?
Frankly, I don't want to be caught
Don't ever love him more that he loves you, is the lesson he's taught

I'm enjoying being chased,
Enjoying running this race
Enjoying the carefree ease of your lies
Wearing love's army fatigues as a disguise
Enjoying my freedom

The last injury I received is taking longer to heal, I'm cruising through the rehabilitation
process just fine
While you keep trying to penetrate the defense line
I love loving me more than trying to love you
More than chasing the pot of gold at the end of the rainbow
And as I listen to the echoes of earnest pleas for my affections
I wonder if it's your erection that guides your image this way

I harden even more because all I can think is- I'm running now, the faster I go the more
you want
I'm being hunted but if I stop, I'll no longer receive the desired effects of the chase

You won't have the same craving
Trapped and then devoured as you take advantage of my weakened position

I won't thrill you anymore
I won't excite you anymore
I won't be appealing any longer
That's why I won't let you love me

Nightspares

Why do I prefer to hug my dreams at night?
Make love to my own passions
To snuggle up with my goals
I hate the game
I hate the lies, the disrespect

Love always disappoints me
Become nightmares, shatters my future, creates scary bedtime stories in an otherwise
cozy place

Taps into my clothing of emotions that I thought I had out grown
I prefer to write about life's lovers, lust, and liars I don't want to be in the game

I'd much rather scribe love into someone else's reality
Leave that shit out of mine
Because it hurts too much

So why do I prefer to hug my dreams at night?
Make love to my own passions?
Lust after success?
And snuggle up with my goals?
Because I hate the game

Because allowing someone to participate in my dreams always results in nightmares

So spare me

Spare me the train wreck

Spare me your negative spirits
Spare me all that horror
Spare me the hurt that demolishes my sole
Spare me the healing process that I cannot control

Love became that monster under my bed that only comes out when I'm in my coziest
place
And I would base
my trust on a liars lust
My fairytales always ended with a loving prince as a must
But I had placed my trust
in a monster in my bed that didn't deserve my passion,
Wore on my spirit
And created my nightspares

Loves Ride

When the pain takes you on a wild ride, an unexpected horror
You tend to not want to climb aboard ever again
Your life becomes a stuttering mess of repetitive sin

So you ride other rides never becoming attached

No desire to love
More desires to lust
Lost all consideration, lost all motivation to trust
Giving and not receiving
Puts you in a state of disconnect
A spirit of disconnect
So you unplug yourself from having a whole life
Glad you're not someone's wife
because that would mean you'd have to forgive and trust
Parts of you work at its full capacity
Other parts find it safe not to feel
To you, no love relationship is real...still you play
You lapse into a love numbing coma, just enjoying the moment
But at what moment do you trust?

Not at this moment, you prefer lust

How much are you suppose to take?
How many times can your heart be pieced back after it breaks?
How many times are you suppose to get back in the game?
They all look the same
You place yourself in direct danger because it feels better than trusting.....lusting is the
superficial fix....it doesn't hurt you

As the misuse goes on for so long

You wonder if any of them will ever belong

Hey baby, what's your name?
See y'all all begin to look the same

You all cheat, you all deceive
And all I'm gonna' receive,
is a wild ride through tunnels of lies
Over mirages of care
Under tracks of pain and despair

So I don't want to ride no more

Ego Trippin'

Your ego is shot cause a peon like me let you go
So I'm writing this piece to let you know
You have the problem I don't
Cause what I use to do, now I won't
I came like a true friend
You came in got what you needed and made like wind

A see saw goes up and down
But it was all about you when you came to town
Teetering in the middle helped you get supplies
Through it all you played just enough for a real lovers lies
But I'm going to always be a true friend
Cause where I am you've never been
I'll give time to those who know how to use friendship
Cause a lot of abused abandoned wanna bes ain't really equipped
They don't know how to give or receive love
So sorry, I've moved on, that ain't my issue
Cause during your tough times I saw you through

And since no one else had ever done that for you
You thought it meant that I was your fool
Well guess what baby, I've moved on, no hard feelings, we still cool
We never was tight no way
I thought so at one point, but not after hearing what you had to say
I allowed you to lean on me
At the time I couldn't see
But baby God opened my eyes and I've set you free

I don't regret it, I'm blessed
Now you acting all brand new, calling me stressed

Cause I caught the vibe and moved on
I knew what you were all about, I just played along

I ain't trippen' though
All that you did I've released and let go
See that's what happened when I wrote this piece
Your using behind has now been released

Cold calculating culprits
Hurt with horrible hands
Exits into
Abnormal allegiance
To tombs of tasteless traps
Effortless examples of an extras emptiness
Reachers of ruining wretchedness
Sorry, simple seekers of subhuman standards

Ping Pong

She was the trophy
Batted back and forth like a ping pong ball
Competitors competing to be the best at banging
Winner receives bragging rights as the trophy sets her sights on the next game

To her, all they were, were skilled marksmen with different stroking styles and after
a while it's time to move on to the next match each competitor becomes emotionally
attached but they were judged for stamina and creativity

For the competitors, banners and trophies reflect their need to flex

For her the posters advertising the victory weren't necessary but no real care on her part

She's hit back and forth
Then caught in a net
She's the sexy center of two opponents bet
She's never been hit hard or knocked off the table
She's never been in a relationship that's healthy or stable

She lands on her back and hits the floor
As one of her opponents makes a score

Top scorer puts in the better hits but
She decides when the game will quit

She let's them think they're in control
But she's only playing a superficial role
It's all a little game of fun
And each can think that they have won

The winner receives bragging rights as

the trophy sets her sights on the next game

Oh No He Didn't!

The party was slamming! It had a beautiful back drop right next to a pool that extended out towards the ocean. Tall beautiful mountains filled the scenery and to top it all off there were plenty of what seemed to be quality male prospects. Eva was looking for some fun. She wore her short shorts that night because she wanted to wear something that screamed, "I'm available but don't push me into the pool." She had just gotten her hair done and it was a $125 hair do and she didn't want it messed up. She hadn't been at the party long before a tall, handsome young man approached. "Hi, you look lonely can I stand next to you?" in a voice somewhat soft for a man. Eva thought, what a dork, but when she looked up at him, she saw this 6 foot 5 inch tall, athletically built caramel mound of excellence! She thought to herself this is going to be HER night! "I guess you can stand anywhere you'd like." Eva responded, not wanting to show how impressed she was with his appearance and trying to come across as cool.

He began the conversation, "So how do you know Carl?" Carl was the host of the party and they were celebrating Carl's birthday at a mansion he'd rented for the weekend.

"He is my personal trainer" Eva said, eager to let him know that she worked out too. She had already checked out his caramel colored baldhead, the gold earring, chiseled pecks, muscular calves, size 13 shoe and the pearly white smile. She examined everything from his head to his toes in just one quick glance. She suspected that he was probably younger than she was because his voice was somewhat light for a man and he didn't seem very confident. "So what's your name?" he said.

"Eva, Eva Houser, so how old are you anyway?" she wanted to get straight to the point. He sounded like her little sister.

"I'm 22", he responded. Eva almost passed out. She was 31 years old but she looked very young. Her first thoughts were to tell him he was just a baby and to go and find another playmate because he was just so much younger than she was. She decided not to reveal her true age just yet and she hoped he didn't ask her. It might be interesting to spend time with a younger man. Eva was the CEO of her own company and she had become very successful but she'd left little time for fun in her life. She owned her own home and was pursuing her Ph. D in business. She was aggressive and always set high goals for herself and she thought he might be a nice "recreational activity".

Derrick had quite the opposite thought process when it came to objectives and goals he lacked the ambitious go for it attitude that Eva had.

"So what do you do?" Eva asked. "For a living I mean," she added later to make it clear what she meant by her question.

"I work for Groceries Plus," he replied. Eva just assumed he held some sort of management or marketing position with the grocery store so she didn't ask what his occupation was. After several hours of dancing, small talk and a few hour derves Eva began to get tired and yawned to let Derrick know she was about to leave. If he wanted more conversations with her now was the time for him to ask for her phone number.

"I'm tired, I have to get up in the morning to go to early church services. I think I'm going to go home." Eva said.

"Let me walk you to your car," Derrick seemed eager and Eva thought, great I guess he'll ask for my number while we're walking.

"So Eva, can I call you sometimes?" he spoke so softly he sounded as though his feelings would have been hurt if she'd said no but Eva was eager to give him her telephone number. She was thinking he seems like a great guy. He stopped near a small round car that was made of mostly glass. She thought to herself this is such a tiny vehicle for such a large man, it must be very uncomfortable for him to drive this thing. It resembled the Pope Mobile. He got some paper and a writing pen from his glove compartment and looked at Eva. "It's 902-426-0000. " Eva responded quickly because she really was ready to go.

The next time Eva went to the spa she asked her personal trainer, Carl, about Derrick and Carl had nothing but positive things to say about him. After Eva had known Derrick for several months he invited her to his apartment for a date. She told him no hanky panky. Of course, this was still the "play hard to get stage" of the friendship and he seemed harmless. He rented an efficiency apartment in an affluent section of the city. It was neat but had meager resources inside of it. They ate on paper plates, used plastic forks and knives and sat on wicker furniture. Eva began to ask common questions. "So Derrick where did you go to school?", Eva opens up the dialogue.

"Oh I went to Mickey Leland", he responded. Mickey Leland? Eva thought, that's a high school.

"No, I mean where did you attend college?" she asked in a sincere tone.

"Oh, I went to San Antonio Junior Work Achievement but I didn't finish." he responded. Eva picked up some embarrassment in his tone, so she tried to make him feel comfortable and she didn't want him to think she was a snob.

"Oh, O.K. that's cool, I understand that," Eva really didn't know what to say and what she had just said didn't go with the conversation they were having. She thought to herself he's a nice guy for now but he shouldn't be considered for a long-term relationship. She was going to keep her emotions in check. No I love yous here. Ambition turned her on! Her man didn't have to have a whole lot of material possessions or have a college education but he had to dream big and work towards the goals he set for himself. Derrick seemed to change his goals regularly but she liked the fact that he said he was a Christian. This was the asset she clinged to when she thought of the Pope Mobile, the tiny apartment, and the lack of focus towards any particular goal. It helped that he was fine too. He sacked groceries at the local grocery store and rarely discussed what he wanted to do beyond that. He had taken some college courses but dropped out before he could complete his degree. He could hold very intelligent conversations. One week he was going to be an airline pilot and the next an attorney. Eva decided it was probably the age difference and excused his extreme thoughts because she wasn't really looking for a husband, she was looking for a good time.

One night while Eva watched television and Derrick prepared dinner a Girls Gone Foul commercial briefly got their attention. He quickly responded, "I John 3:4 states that whoever commits sin transgresses for sin is the transgression of the law." Eva thought, he sure knows the Bible well and that impressed her. Derrick walks over and puts the plates on the table. They said their grace for dinner then began to eat the meal that he had prepared for them. The meal looked delicious, everything was neatly placed on the paper plates and she could tell that he was very serious about his culinary creations because he garnished their meal with parsley and lemon wedges. How many men would take the time to put garnish on his dates plate for a meal for two at home? This was nice Eva thought to herself. The food was good but the conversation was very different from what Eva was used to. When Eva would bring up social issues that were important to her, issues like world hunger, for example, he would say something silly and completely non-related to the topic. Eva said, "There's enough resources to wipe out hunger in this world, especially on the continent of Africa".

His response to her comment was; do you want me to drive my car over there and feed them? His comments were playful and very non-sarcastic. His playfulness was great sometimes or even most of the time but it could become annoying because it seemed that he could never have a serious conversation. Eva needed intellectual as well as physical stimulation and he wasn't meeting that need during this date. She thought O.K. it's just the first date maybe he's nervous maybe it will get better but it didn't get better. He did silly things like holding her down then licking her face, putting a large amount of saliva on her, or pinning her under a blanket with him while he passed gas. She looked over his lack of funds and his immaturity to explore the positive qualities he had. Her encounters with men lately had been unfavorable. After all there wasn't a whole lot of eligible dates out there, they were either married, jobless or something else was wrong with them. Several weeks later Eva needed a dress for a relatives wedding so she and Derrick went to the mall together.

Several teenagers passed them rather scantily dressed and Derrick quoted another scripture, "1 Thessalonians 4:3-6 says it is God's will that you should be holy; that you should avoid sexual immorality; that each of you should learn to control his own body in a way that is holy and honorable, not in passionate lust like the heathen". Yet Eva noticed he couldn't take his eyes off their behinds. Eva thought I really like that he knows the word of God and a real man is going to look. While Eva and Derrick held hands and continued to walk through the shopping mall Eva saw a dress in the window of a department store. The dress fit the mannequin snuggly and it had a low cut front and back, the very revealing style caught their eyes. Derrick and Eva stopped to admire the dress. "Eva you need to do something about your weight." Derrick said very matter of factly. Eva was astonished that Derrick would criticize her weight since she had lost 5 pounds and he'd gained 10.

The following week Eva had gone to the hair salon and decided to change the style of her hair to a more curly look. Derrick didn't approve of the hairstyle change but he never mentioned the dislike for her new hairstyle while they were alone together but he decided to purposely embarrass Eva while she chatted with her neighbors outside her home. "So Eva why did you make your hair into a big disco ball?" and then stood there waiting for others to laugh at her. Her feelings were hurt and she was embarrassed. She was angry but held her thoughts, because she planned to deal with him later. She hated public embarrassments.

Holidays with Derrick really irked Eva the most. On Valentine's Day Derrick went to her house where she'd made a candle lit dinner, she bought Derrick a Movado watch and he responded to her generosity by telling her he already had a watch and then asked her why would she buy him another one. She thought he'd stop his ungrateful comments when he saw how hurt her feeling were. Her facial expressions told him just how hurt she was but he chose to ask her, "What made you think I'd want this?" several more times. A Movado watch was very expensive and his reaction hurt Eva's feelings but she was also thinking maybe he got her something very exquisite since he complained about her gift. It was silly of her to think that someone with his income could give her a lavish gift but he had insulted her by complaining about what she'd given him, surely he'd gotten a gift for Eva that was more elaborate than the watch. He handed her a used stuffed animal and a broken crystal clock. She was furious but had too much class to show it, she said thank you in a soft voice but in her mind she was thinking is this another one of his jokes? No, he was serious. Eva was the type of person who addressed issues after she calmed down for fear of burning bridges and alleviating herself of the guilt she felt when she thought she'd hurt another persons feelings wrongly.

As time went on Eva taught herself to look over all of Derrick's shortcomings and focus on his positive qualities. He was very sensitive. While at first that turned her off she learned to appreciate his caring demeanor. So many men that Eva dated had been mean and lacked values. Rather than see his playfulness as foolishness she embraced his sense of humor. Eva's business required her to be highly visible in public and her position was stressful so his lighthearted playfulness became a pleasant break from her everyday monotony. She enjoyed him. His cooking was a bonus for Eva since she really couldn't cook well at all but his inability to ever be serious was a major turn off. She needed intellectual stimulation. She wanted to have a serious conversation with him and he didn't appear capable of having one. She began to want to go on a real date for a change and she knew he couldn't afford that. She began to notice more of his hypocritical manner. He would say "Matthew 15:19 and 20 says out of the heart come evil thoughts, murder, adultery, sexual immorality" and then he'd breathe down Eva's neck almost constantly pleading with her for sex. Eva felt guilty every time she and Derrick had sex since they both were trying to live Christian lives.

One night Derrick called and invited her to his apartment for dinner. "Hey Leave-a-Eva", he'd made up a nickname for her, which she hated, "I've got your favorite-baked chicken, rice and green beans", she thought, I don't even like green beans but she was hungry and his offer to share a balanced meal with her was right on time, "Why don't you come over here?" he said in a very pleasant voice. Excited that he'd offered because she wasn't the best cook, she thought, cool I'll be there. His apartment was at least a 45-minute drive from her house in Madelen Heights but she was willing to make that trip for a good meal. When she arrived he'd set the table with candles and personally picked fresh flowers, plastic wineglasses with some sort of very inexpensive wine and now plastic plates rather than paper plates this time. She had become tired of the same old dates time after time but she appreciated the effort he'd put into their dates and after about 7 months of dating he seemed to love her. She had grown to like him a lot in spite of all the shortcomings he had, she often told herself "I'm not perfect either and who is?" When they finished eating dinner, Derrick came over to Eva's side of the table and began to kiss her. He began with her lips, then lightly around her neck then to her breast. She weakened and they made love on the floor that night, Derrick didn't have a bed. Not 10 minutes after Derrick and Eva made love, Derrick made an urgent call from midair or from space or maybe he had telepathy but whatever it was all of a sudden this urgent phone call sent him into a frenzy, he had to take a flight out to Austin, Texas right away. He ran to put on his clothes without even taking a shower then rushed her out the door. "Eva, I've got to go take care of this." Eva thought to herself that is the most unrealistic load of crap she had ever seen or heard. He's a terrible liar, he makes a phone call, it becomes urgent and now he must run out on her. "He's cheating!" she thought to herself, I don't really like him anyway so this will be the perfect opportunity to break up with him. This little peon! All the exceptions she'd made. She'd looked over all of his foolishness but not this time.

The next day she called him, "So Derrick you had an emergency yesterday?" she asked in a cynical but calm voice. He knew where she was taking the conversation because her voice had a hint of anger.

"Well, uh, yea, uh, why are you asking me all that?" he responded

"Asking you all of what? I asked you one simple question!" Eva responded forcefully.

"You're always asking me questions," he sounded as if he were about to cry, his voice cracked.

"I tell you what, this isn't working for me so why don't you just move around. I'm not interested in seeing you anymore!" Eva finished her sentence and hung up the phone. She was feeling hurt but she also was glad she had gotten rid of him. She had become tired of his cheap dates, foolish ways and ungratefulness anyway but there was still this since of loss. He had taken up a lot of her free time and now she was on the 'market' again, back into the dating game. She really hated the instability that came with dating. First, the awkward period of getting to know a new guy, then finding out he's not right for her and then starting all over again with a new friend.

She didn't waste any time, though, she began taking those second looks at potential dates again. She met a guy at a gas station. He had a nice car, the new 350 Sports Mercedes Benz, red, her favorite color. "Hi," he said in an unusually deep voice. Somehow Eva felt that he was adding some extra base tone to his voice to flex his masculinity or something. She wasn't sure why he would do something so juvenile as to change his voice while he was speaking to her.

"Oh, hi", she responded.

"You're looking great in those jeans. Can I call you sometimes?" he asked.

Eva hesitated, stared at him for a few minutes and because she just broke up with Derrick she thought this new guy might be a good distraction.

"Yea, O.K." He might be good for a date; she thought to herself. He gets in his car and begins to reach for his glove compartment when he caught a glimpse of himself in his rear view mirror. Eva thought he was going to get out and hand her his business card or something but he sat in front of his mirror for the next 10 minutes admiring himself. When Eva finished pumping gas into her vehicle she got in her car and left him still sitting, admiring himself. Eva thought out loud, "I can't date anyone who thinks he's prettier than I am."

Eva worked out regularly and she met new people at the gym all the time. One evening after work she went into the gym, still in her business suit from her job and carrying her gym bag. She walked pass a lot of new faces but most of them familiar. The gym was like a big family, everyone had been exercising there for many years so they knew each other well. She was eager to get into her gym attire and start her workout. When she finished dressing, she walked out of the dressing room and quickly moved towards the scale to weigh herself, when an older gentleman bumped into her. "Gosh, you almost knocked me down!" the older gentleman said in a somewhat playful voice.

Eva rolled her eyes at him, she found him amusing, "Please man, I didn't almost knock you down. You need to move away from the scale anyway, I don't need anyone seeing how much I weigh!"

"How much do you weigh? 180 pounds, 175?" he started playfully with Eva.

"Please, step away from the scale!" Eva said loudly and slowly as if she was imitating a police officer yelling at a criminal. He began to laugh.

"What's your name?" he asked.

"Eva," she replied.

"I'm Tony" he said in a crackly voice.

"Well nice to meet you Tony". Eva had no interest in Tony, but she could tell by his demeanor that he was looking for something more than the short conversation they were having at that moment.

"I've never seen you here before." he continued to want to talk.

"Well, I'm here a lot, usually I work late so I come here later in the day. Today was an unusually light day at work so that's why I'm here now." Eva said really fast wanting to get into her workout and hoping he'd pick up the hint that she really didn't want to talk anymore. Her quick talking and her movements to walk away from him should have been enough.

"I hope to see you again sometimes, Eva" he said in a very flirtatious manner. Eva thought to herself, is he kidding? No way would I ever date someone whose old enough to be my dad. Yuck! But as time went by she'd see Tony often at the gym, they'd talk about various topics. She soon discovered that he was a very nice guy and Eva had a lot of things in common with Tony. They both loved fine arts. Tony was a singer, painter, sculptor and photographer. Eva took fine arts classes for fun nothing professionally though, Tony did this professionally. Eva began to find Tony quite interesting. Eventually Tony asked her out for dinner and she agreed. They began to go out regularly but as time went on Tony wanted her to come over to his house everyday, listen to him sing and then he wanted to have sex. Eva thought to herself, is he taking Viagra? My God he just keeps pawing me like an animal in heat! I've got to let him go, I can't date him anymore. They both understood that they weren't in a deeply committed relationship anyway. So

Eva told Tony she didn't think it was working out and that they shouldn't see one another intimately. They remained friends but no longer dated. Every now and then Tony would call Eva to see if she'd changed her mind about having sex with him but she truly didn't have a desire to be with him.

Months went by and Eva went about her life without dating anyone. She was visiting her family one day when an old childhood friend stopped by her parent's house while she was there. His family was really good friends with her family. His mother was sending Eva's mother a recipe for a new chicken casserole she'd made. There was a knock at the door and Eva answered. "Hi, Jeff," Eva said excitedly because she was seeing her old childhood friend.

"Hi Eva. Your mom wanted this recipe my mom sent this." Jeff spoke well and handed Eva a crumpled piece of paper. She noticed how handsome he was now. He had changed from the skinny little kid with glasses and braces on his teeth. He was now tall and slim with a beautiful smile.

"Come on in," Eva said kindly.

"Sure, but I can't stay long. I've got to get to the airport. I'm flying to Chicago to meet some friends. We're just going to be hanging out." Jeff replied.

"Oh, that is so cool. I love to travel. I'd like to go to Chicago one day. The Windy City. Well have a good time." Eva was sincere about encouraging him to enjoy himself. She loved to travel and have a good time too.

"Well I have to go. Eva call me sometime. Your mom has my number. I'm back at home with my mom." Jeff got up to leave, he gave Eva a hug and then he left. Before the week was over Jeff called Eva. He was still in Chicago, he told her he was just wanting to say hello and that he enjoyed seeing her the other day. Eva thought O.K. this is looking good. He's calling, maybe we'll get together when he comes back. As soon as Jeff got back into town he called Eva again. "Eva, it's Jeff, it was so nice seeing you. What are you doing tonight?"

"I don't have anything planned. Why what do you have going on?" Eva asked.

"I was wondering if you'd like to hang out with me at Pete's Place? Me and couple of my friends and their wives are going. We'll be leaving at about 6 .p.m. " Jeff replied.

"Sure, that sounds great to me." Eva got off the phone She felt really good about the encounters she was having with Jeff. They'd grown up in the same neighborhood, their families were the best of friends, and Jeff had a lot going for him. He was an officer in the U.S. Air Force, he had a college degree in mechanical engineering and he knew how to dress well. She loved his ambition, he was always setting high goals for himself and working towards them. The dates he'd plan were always fun and interesting but Jeff would disappear for days at a time. Eva wouldn't hear from him at all. If she called him he wouldn't answer his cellular phone and he wouldn't be at his mother's home either. When he did finally contact her he'd always say the same thing. Oh, I went and met some friends and it would always be in some other state that he'd go to meet these 'friends'. Eva believed him since she had no reason not to trust what he was telling her, besides he was very kind to her and he would look into her eyes when he responded to her questions. Jeff would get Eva anything she wanted. Eva wouldn't even ask him for any material things, but if he over heard her say she liked something he'd go right out to a department store and surprise her with it. Eva believed Jeff liked her very much. One night Eva went to a jazz club with friends. It was a popular downtown hang out and while she was there she saw Jeff. "I thought he was out of town with friends," Eva said to her girlfriends she had gone to the club with, her friends started to stare at the loving couple sitting on the other side of the bar. Jeff and his date were giving each other little short kisses, smiling at each other, feeding each other and talking. Eva approached the loving couple. "Hi Jeff, thought you were out of town. I see you're right here though." Eva said in an angry voice.

"Oh Eva this is Mary Ann, Uh I just got back into town." Jeff said nervously.

"Well don't call me anymore O.K. Jeff," Eva walked away. She was angry, even though she wasn't really in love with him she didn't like the lies he'd told. He could have been more honest with her and she could've accepted dating him even if he did see other women because Eva believed that two people could date each other and date other people also as long as they were honest about it. Before Eva left the jazz club with her friends another woman had walked up to Jeff and threw a drink in his face, apparently Jeff was unzipping his pants all over the place and it was catching up with him that night. Jeff called Eva several times to try to explain his situation but Eva never spoke to him again.

Then there was the coupon cutter, buy one get one free guy. She met him at the neighborhood grocery store. Eva noticed him as he shopped because he was a fairly handsome looking guy. If she had any interest in a guy and he was shopping she always paid close attention to the items he was purchasing, if he was shopping alone. The items in a man's grocery basket could tell her a lot about who he was. She noticed several frozen pizzas, a number of ready made dinners, several bags of chips and packages of cookies. He must be single she thought. He wasn't wearing a wedding band either. As he went to pay for his groceries she ended up behind him at the check out counter. As he put his groceries on the moving conveyer belt she noticed his envelope of coupons. Wow, a man whose thrifty with his money. She decided to make a comment just to began some sort of dialogue with him. "So, I see you have the Fajita Chicken Dijorno Pizza, I've never had that before is it good?" Eva asked. Her intent was to get him to talk to her.

"Oh, yeeesss", he extended the yes to emphasize his like for this type of pizza.

"I need to try it sometime", Eva responded. By this time the cashier totaled his items and he seemed to have a coupon for each item that he'd purchased. The cashier began with $22.61 and after she finished entering his coupons into her cash register his total grocery purchase was $14.12. This gave Eva something else to say. "Wow, you saved about $6 that's pretty good."

"Yea, I love saving money," he said. Eva loved saving money too but she thought coupons were too cumbersome and besides they didn't usually have coupons for the brand names of items she preferred to buy. As the cashier began to slide Eva's groceries one by one across the scanner light Eva noticed that he was still putting his unused coupons in his pocket and reviewing his receipt. He was searching for any mistakes the cashier may have made but she also sensed that he may have been delaying his walk out the door because he wanted to chat with her more or at least this is what she was hoping he was doing. She pushed her basket ahead and he said, "How'd you like to eat pizza with me and a group of my friends, the games coming on tonight and every bodies bringing something?" Eva thought I really don't know this guy but he seems nice and harmless.

"Can I bring a friend?" she asked. Not wanting to go to a strange persons house alone but not wanting to miss out on the fun either.

"Sure, is this friend a girl or a guy?" he said, winking at her to let her know that he had a romantic interest in her and implying that she shouldn't bring a guy.

She responded with a flirtatious grin on her face, "It's a girl."

"Oh, bring some chips, a case of soda, ketchup, mustard and a package of hot dog buns." he responded very quickly after she accepted his invitation. "Here's my number, by the way my name's Fred and here are the directions to my house." While he was writing his information down to give to her, Eva thought that sure is a lot to ask of someone you just met; bring what? She didn't even get the whole list. She decide to just respond as though she got all the requested party foods he had just rattled off to her. "O.K. sure," she said and she walked away. She thought to herself I won't be seeing him again. Eva didn't mind bringing an item or 2 to contribute to a gathering but she thought it was a bit much to ask for all of that from a person he'd just met. She was a guest not the host. The coupons, scrutinizing the receipt, asking her to bring 5 grocery items to his party gave her all the indications that he was probably selfish and self centered so she never contacted him and she never went the gathering that day either. She thought, no love lost here.

The next day was Monday and Monday mornings were always hard for Eva. She tried to relax and truly enjoy her weekends but her body still wanted to sleep when the 6 a.m. alarm went off. Work was always more intense on Mondays too. She had six new project leads she needed to pursue and develop. Her livelihood was based on her ability to successfully accomplish a number of set goals. She began her day with a large cup of coffee from Starbucks and she drove an hour commute to her office. She entered into the building, unlocked her office with her keys, turned the lights on, sat her purse and coffee down, and when she turned back around there was a tall man standing behind her. She was startled. "May I help you?" she tried not to sound frightened but she was.

"Uh, yes I'm looking for a Miss Houser, I'd like to apply for the job as a personal assistant." he said realizing her nervousness he tried to speak as pleasantly as he could and make his intentions known right away.

"Oh yes may I see your resume?" Eva said calmly, realizing he wasn't a threat but he was there to respond to the newspaper add she put out requesting a personal assistant. "Please, have a seat. O.K. Mr. Paul Bennett you seem to have several years of experience, " Eva flipped the pages of his resume, she knew all of his former supervisors. She followed up on 2 of his references and then hired him almost immediately. They worked long hours together. Eventually they became friends, then lovers and later married. The marriage didn't work out. She and Paul had come from 2 totally different backgrounds. Eva had 2 educated parents who had been married for 35 years while Paul grew up with a single mother who struggled to get him through college. While Eva admired that part of her husband the most, the fact that he had come from such challenging circumstances and became successful in spite of that, it was also the very thing that drove them away from one another. She saw life very differently than he did. They fought a lot about basic things such as how to pay the bills, whether or not to turn the air conditioning on when it was 100 degrees outside and even how to cook their meals. They knew they needed to leave each other in order to be happy so eventually they divorced after 4 years of marriage. Paul took more than half the company she had built leaving Eva in a very different financial position. She eventually had to sell the house, get a smaller more economically priced car and cut her budget everywhere. No more long vacations, or expensive trips to the day spa, she had to start all over again. Eva went back to using her last name again after the divorce. Eva had just had it with the love game. She decided to stop taking life so seriously and to just let life come as it should. Enjoying whatever God gives!

THREE YEARS LATER

One Sunday after church while Eva was leaving she heard a voice yelling out to her. "Hey Leave-a-Diva", she would know that voice anywhere it was Derrick. She turned around and sure enough there he was.

"Hey, Derrick how are you? What have you been up to?", Eva said without letting him answer the first question. They hugged briefly and then looked into each others eyes as if they were studying each other.

"Oh, I've been doing O.K." he didn't sound like things were going too well with him by the sudden change in his voice. He spoke softer and looked down.

Eva knew things weren't all that great just by his response, "So are you married?"

"No Eva I'm divorced, she left me" Derrick said. She could hear the pain in his voice. He must still be getting over her Eva thought to herself. Wow, he still looks the same, tall and fine, a little larger than he was years ago but still fine.

"I'm sorry to hear that. Are you O.K.?" Eva tried to sound empathetic and she actually was empathetic to a small extent.

"Yes, I'm fine. I've thought about you a lot but I didn't know if I should contact you. I didn't know if you were married," Derrick said.

"Well I'm divorced too." Eva had a sound of happiness in her voice. She had learned to love being single and she didn't take dating very seriously anymore. She enjoyed not being in love. Being in love for Eva meant someone was going to interrupt her fun. She could travel on a whim. She was comfortable not having to explain where she was going and where she'd been. She didn't spend a lot of time on where the last guy she dated was after the date was over either. It was almost like an out of sight-out of mind reaction to any of the guys she came in contact with. She preferred dating rather than searching for this serious boyfriend or getting her feelings hurt because she thought this guy was the one but each one of them turned out to be a loser time and time again. She enjoyed her life. She felt like she was in a good place at that moment. She had truly found fulfillment in all the things that God had blessed her with. Even though her finances were not the best at that time, she knew it was a temporary setback. The divorce had left her struggling to regain the level of income that she had once before become accustom to. Still she had peace of mind and she had begun to pursue all the things in her life that she wanted rather than needed to do. She was taking music, dance, painting and sculpting classes. She had joined a missionary group and had begun to travel to very exotic places. She found fulfillment in helping others through the missionary group that organized each trip. She wasn't interested in a serious relationship at all because she was happy where she was right then. "Why don't we go to brunch? I know this great place just down the street from here. Come on ride with me and I'll drop you back off at your car when we're done eating." Derrick's voice sounded so pleasant, she couldn't resist.

"Sure, that would be fine." Eva responded. Eva followed Derrick to his car. It was a new silver Jaguar. Eva wasn't expecting to see Derrick in such an expensive vehicle because when they dated 6 years before he didn't have much of an income and he wasn't really pursuing a better lifestyle for himself. They got to the restaurant and were seated immediately. Derrick begins the conversation.

"Eva, wow you look the same" Derrick said. "You look great. I've thought about you a lot, and I really want to be in a serious relationship. You know what I mean. I want to love someone fully, with my whole heart and I want them to love me back. Eva, I want a traveling companion, a real partner." During the first few minutes of the conversation he expressed how he really wanted a 'real' relationship. He didn't want to date anyone else just her. "I missed you Eva." Derrick begins.

"Well why did you cheat on me?" Eva asked somewhat angrily.

"Cheat! I never cheated on you Eva! What are you talking about?" Derrick was aggitated. "Had you just communicated with me you'd have known the truth. I didn't cheat!"

"Derrick please that magical phone call remember that? Running out the door on me! Please! I was sure it was another woman." Eva replied in an untrusting voice.

"Had you just communicated that you'd have known that my dad was sick and I needed to get home right away." Derrick said softly trying to calm the situation. "Eva, I've thought about you a lot and I want you back. Just you and me baby let's try it again?"

Eva thought to herself yea right he's just like all the rest of them, he says one thing and does something totally different. He's probably dating other women all over the place. Eva had become so cynical because of her divorce and past dating experiences but she didn't say any of her thoughts out loud. He's just saying that because he can't stand the thought of the woman he's with being with someone else. He probably has a lot of problems too and she didn't want to allow that to affect her life in a negative way. "This is so fast, we haven't seen each other in years, we've both changed, how do you know you want to date me?"

"It's not like we don't already know each other Eva!" Derrick said with frustration.

"I really don't have time for a serious relationship. I enjoy dating. We can just have a good time no strings attached." Eva expressed her true feelings about their relationship right away.

"I'm not interested in that at all. I'm looking for a real partner. I want someone to travel with, I want to know that person has my back when times get tough, I want a monogamous relationship." Eva had been through so much, she listened to Derrick but the whole time he was talking she was thinking this is a load of manure, he's just like all the rest of them he doesn't want a real relationship he's probably got women everywhere. Why won't he just come clean and tell the truth? Why does he have to lye about seeing other women? We aren't married but she didn't verbally express herself as bluntly as she was feeling.

"Well, I just want to date. I really don't want a serious relationship." and as bluntly as Eva expressed herself.

Derrick responded just as directly as she did, "Well I'm not looking for that!"

Eva thought right then this would probably be there last encounter. She remembered what happened years before with the mysterious phone call and his abrupt departure from her that seemed to be some sort of lye he was telling to her to get away from her. It sure seemed like he was going to another woman.

They left brunch that day with mixed feelings. They were both glad that they'd seen each other but they were pursuing 2 different relationship paths. Derrick seemed to want a serious relationship and he wanted it right away. He didn't want to waste anytime reacquainting himself with Eva. It had been 8 years since they'd seen each other and surely they'd both changed. Eva had been disappointed by a series of relationship experiences so she wanted to take her time before she even considered Derrick as a serious boyfriend. Derrick seemed to have experienced that one failed relationship, his marriage, so he was eager to begin a new relationship. She didn't expect Derrick to call her again because they weren't pursuing the same relationship goals. They left the restaurant together, he took her back to her car, they had a very long hug and said their goodbyes.

Two weeks later Eva received a phone call from Derrick. "Hey Leava-A- Eva. What's going on with you?" His voice sounded cheerful as though he'd erased from his memory the entire conversation they had had at the restaurant previously. "What are you doing today? I've got some tickets to a baseball game. Why don't you come join me?"

Eva kind of knew he'd call back even though he acted as though he wouldn't speak to her again because she didn't want a serious relationship with him right away.

"Sure I'd love to go, Derrick." Eva had only gone to 3 professional baseball games in her entire life so this would be a great experience for her. When Derrick picked Eva up, he had an extra matching baseball jersey and hat for her to wear to the game.

"Wow, thanks Derrick this is very nice of you!" Eva was really impressed with his thoughtful gesture. When they got to the baseball stadium Eva soon realized that Derrick was a season ticket holder and that they had reserved box seats. Derrick ordered a bottle of champagne, a variety of finger foods and soft drinks. It was obvious he was trying to impress her and he was definitely succeeding. He took Eva to her apartment that night, kissed her on the cheek, told her he'd had a great time and that he looked forward to doing that again and then he left. He didn't make her feel as though she owed him something after the date and that really made her feel good.

Eva had to sell her home after her divorce and she was now living in a small apartment. She also placed herself on a strict budget, which meant no frivolous spending. She never asked men for money because she had been taught by her parents not to do that-ever. Don't even accept expensive gifts. When you ask a man for money he thinks he owns you and he's going to expect sex from you, her mother would always say, so she never asked Derrick to give her money but as time went on Eva and Derrick spent more time together. She noticed that Derrick had become more mature and wasn't making the foolish comments that he'd regularly made when they dated previously. He didn't critique her appearance anymore. She began to test Derrick. She purposely wore a mismatched colored blouse with a pair of colorful pants, socks and sandals and didn't comb her hair perfectly in an effort to see if Derrick would criticize her or attempt to embarrass her in front of other people. He just said O.K. let's go to the store. She was shocked, wow this is different. It was like she was dating a completely different person this time.

One evening Derrick asked Eva out for dinner. He took her to a downtown dinner, jazz club where they ate good food, listened to great music and laughed most of the night. He then suprised her by taking her to one of the most expensive hotels in the city. Their hotel room window overlooked the cities beautiful skyline. "Derrick I'm not prepared to stay over night. I don't have any clothes and I need some toiletries." Eva was sceptical but felt that everything Derrick was doing was awesome. She loved his spontonaity. Derrick picked up the phone and called the consiare. "Yes this is room 1304 would you bring us some ladies toiletries please. Yes, thank you very much." Eva was in heaven. This was just the kind of man she'd always dreamed of. She would have never expected Derrick to grow to this point. Eva even enjoyed the bowling and pizza dates. He'd plan the dates out well and they'd laugh and talk, make jokes about the way the other person bowled and kissed between each game. One day Derrick called Eva and told her to clear her schedule completely for the next 4 days and to pack enough clothes for a 4 day excursion. He wouldn't tell her where he was taking her. He picked her up at her apartment and they drove straight to the airport. He surprised Eva with a trip to Cancun. Eva loved it. She was so in love with Derrick. It was as though God had taken them away from each other for a while to help them to grow into the people they are presently. Now they were just right for each other. When they got back into the city after their vacation. Derrick rushed to drop Eva off at her apartment and explained that he had to be at work within the next hour. He pulled up in front of her apartment, gave her a short kiss, then sped off. Eva didn't hear from Derrick for the next 3 days. She'd call his home but she wouldn't get an answer. She'd call his cellular phone and still no answer. Eva began to think something tragic had happened to Derrick until her phone rang 4 days later. "Hey, Leave-a-Eva! What are you up to?" He sounded as though nothing unusual had taken place. Eva was confused and upset.

"Where have you been? I've been calling and calling. I thought something was wrong!" Eva said angrily.

"Oh, baby don't be mad. I was just working." he said in a very sincere tone.

"And you couldn't call to let me know that?" Eva responded, glad that he was in good health and no tragedies had taken place but disappointed at his lack of response to her.

"We've been busy baby. I'll make it up to you." Derrick told her. As time went on Derrick continues to call sparingly. When he did call, Eva was excited. She had come to love Derrick deeply and she was willing to tolerate more this time than she was when they had dated years before. Another 4 days go by when Derrick decides to call Eva again.

"Hey, baby don't be angry, why don't you come over to my place tonight I have a surprise for you." Derrick says softly. By this time Eva is so in love with Derrick that she is just happy he called her at all.

"Sure I'll see you tonight at about 8?" she asked.

"Yea, that sounds good." Derrick tells her. When Eva arrives at Derrick's home she knocks on the door. There was no answer so she knocked again and then she could hear Derrick yell, "Come on in." Eva opened the door slowly. The lights were dim all over the house. Candles were lit everywhere. Soft music was playing and fresh rose peddles made a path through the house up the steps and into Derrick's bathroom where a large round jacuzzi tub sat. Derrick was sitting there with two glasses of champagne. "Take your clothes off he said," in a somewhat demanding tone. Eva said nothing, she began to unbutton her dress and let it drop to the floor. Derrick kept his eyes on her. He looked as though he was going to devoir her. She unsnapped her bra and through it at him and then she slowly removed her panties. She walked towards the jacuzzi and Derrick put his hands around her waist and pulled her close to him. "I love you Eva. Please promise you'll always be here for me. Promise to never cheat on me. Don't ever do that to us. Promise this to me Eva." Derrick sounded so sincere. At that moment Eva believed that she couldn't love anybody more than she loved Derrick.

"I promise Derrick, I'll always love you." Eva spoke in a sexy whisper. All of a sudden there was a loud thump, both Eva and Derrick became very still. They could hear footsteps. The sound of the footsteps became louder and louder, then there was a loud thud. Someone was standing at the bathroom doorway. Eva couldn't tell if it was a man or a woman. It could be a very large woman or an average sized man. Then a deep voice rang out.

"What in the hell are you doing in my house with my husband?" the stout figure yelled out. Then the lights came on. Eva could see a tall, husky tattered looking woman standing at the doorway of the bathroom.

"Husband! This is your husband?" Eva yelled.

"Yea, hoe and what are you doing in my house?" the woman screamed.

"Derrick told me you were divorced." Eva looked over at Derrick who had now jumped out of the tub and was running for his clothes.

"Derrick lied. I'm still his wife and you're in my house!" she told Eva. Eva quickly grabbed her clothes and while she was putting her garments on she could feel her heart breaking. She was devastated. After all of this, he was married. Eva looked at Derrick and all Derrick could say was, "Well, Eva I knew this time was coming. Your financial situation turned me off anyway, so just get your stuff and get out of my house." If Eva hadn't heard it with her own ears she wouldn't have believed it. OH NO HE DIDN'T just tell her that her financial situation had begun to turn him off. When she met him he had nothing and she tolerated that but now she's not good enough and the person who policed everyone elses morals has a wife. OH NO HE DIDN'T!

CHOCOLATE INK

Poetry and prose for poets and writers

Giving Birth to Poetry

From its conception it's my baby to nurture, my thoughts and my ideas, my words
My celebratory child bearing screams to be heard
My family of fellow poets encompassing our delivery room excitement concurred

It grows in my womb becomes life as I put my pen to paper, feed my unseen untouched
baby ballads with adjectives, verbs, nouns and nutritional prepositions
There's a heart beat within these words lay back, relax, listen
To give life to phrases is my poetic mission
Finding pride as each evolutionary stage makes its transition

My ultrasounds display my nouns
As stanzas compound

As the weight of my writing increases so does my need to give birth to verse

My examinations exhibit expansions of exclamations, capitalizations and situations
brought to life

And as I put my pen to paper in an effort to give birth to steamy, sestinas, humorous
haikus, passionate pantoums, sensual sonnets departing my body like cries of sweet
lullabies

Cutting the umbilical cord releasing its attachment to me and allowing my words to
breathe their own breath alone, free

Cradling it, holding it, then giving it a name
A name that means something … that defines its purpose in this world
Stretching itself out from its fetal position curl

Staring into it's beautiful existence my pantoum pearl

Throughout it's childhood I promise to nurture it as it learns to crawl, then walk and
ultimately run
Provide nourishing knowledge because its melodious adolescent existence has just begun
To protect from negative influences so its development won't succumb
And guide it through rough times as our poetic spirits become one

I will nurture my most precious gift as it begins to make sounds, then words, eventually
phrases, then into meaningful independent thoughts
This is what any good poetic parent ought

And as it enters into its adolescent stages, wild carefree and uncensored I'll be careful
to allow my words to have their freedoms but guide and encourage them to take
responsibility for their impact on society
Take special family time to mold and shape their experiences with variety

May these words ripen into strong seasoned syllables stimulating the reflections of life
Encouragements of strength though life's strife

Because real poets don't allow their words to experience premature death
Don't accept a demise that has come from the no talents and wanna-bes
Your living existence, your road to heaven's gate is what they see

Words buried after critics slammed coffin covers
Murdering your zeal their objective to smother

Your voice to be silenced while lying inside a casket of wasted talent
Come back alive, stand tall, hold your head up ....be brave

Ode to Nikki

dedicated to Nikki Giovanni

I was "Kidnapped By a Poet"
Placed in phrases and meters
While there I would vibe off the historical messages
About the revolution and my African heritage
I would seek the edginess of black love in the lines of her words
Her pen would stroke the reflections of the moment
Her moments, My moments
Her paper the resting place for personal inflections paramount to me
She is the poet, the revolutionary, A sista', My sista'
Blazing through relatable roads and pathways to my soul
Vibing on the voices of the movement
Power to the people and the embrace of my ancestors kinks
She would inscribe the spirits of my forefathers into my soul
Paint the struggle into my psyche and from there inspire verse
So down to earth, so me
And as a writer all that I want to be

Poetic Parasites

A part of me was carved from my soul yesterday

My heart was placed on paper and a thief took it, rewrote it, called it theirs as I lay in the operating room of life helpless and trusting

A piece of my poetic flesh was ripped from my gut
and I feel every affect of the cut

As I beg for an anesthetic called a copy write,
still I couldn't prevent the bite
The pain leaves my emotions heavy as dark clouds struggle to stay high but eventually become tears and fall in wet droplets disfiguring my words

I ache as I think of my poetic spirit being sapped from me like a thief stealing body parts just to use as poetic implants in their unimaginative souls

Slicing away at integrity and surgically removing trust

X-rays revealed a broken soul
And further evaluations revealed unethical liars, brazen and bold
But Poetic Parasites aren't in control

A part of me was carved from my soul yesterday

As I come out of the anesthetic, I have to allow myself to feel the after affects of their pen
It feels like I'm dying although my poetic nurses reassure me that I'm not
They've had poetic parasites remove what they've got

They had been here too
So each of them knew exactly what to do
They reassured me I'd get through it

A part of me was carved from my soul yesterday

Poetic Throne

Why do you hate me so?
Because all your poems rhymes
All of it is in a cute little line
And all you can think to do is critique me
If you can't handle Poetic Chocolate don't enter my world
Don't take me home
Don't get me alone
Because this queen sits on the everlasting Poetic Throne
Spittin', Splitten', never Quiten'
I'm going to keep writing what I want to write
I'm just real and that makes "closet sinners" and fake people uncomfortable
I'm going to make it ....I'm going to keep making the fakers uncomfortable
Because I'm going to tell the truth and the truth isn't always pleasant, it's not always
sweet
It's not always neat
In a little line
Some people prefer to remain blind
to the plights that affect human life
Our babies are not always getting what they most assuredly are worth
And I'm going to tell it

Our teenagers are making life changing decisions and I'm going to discuss it
And yes I become angry sometimes and I express it in it's entirety and if my travel
through reality makes you uncomfortable

I have absolutely no apologizes or regrets for you

If you can't handle Poetic Chocolate don't enter my world
Don't pick my words up
Don't follow me home
Don't get me alone
Because this queen sits on that everlasting "Poetic Throne"

Scorned for my words
Shocked by what you've heard?
Good because I must be saying something and it must be penetrating the sores of your
insecure soul
But my pen isn't under your control
Your insults have gotten old
And I've returned, I've returned
with new tracks behind the lyrics
Here, right here to make this thang clear

Puttin' it down
Uniquely and profound with
G's sultry poetic sound

A Vacation From My Life

Can I take a vacation away from my life?
Can I take a vacation away from my life?
Can I go onto a poetic island

                                    or

Fly to a hypnotic continent and just take a vacation from my life?

Can I leave for a minute and not take the pain of my students daily existence with me?

I want to chill
Can I snorkel my way past the coral walls of bills?

Can I get to Poetic Island and just love on the gifts?

Just relax and enjoy the hypno-poetry that soothes my soul.

Can I embrace the warmth of my fellow Poetians?

I just want to take a vacation from my life.
I came to this venue to take a vacation from my life.

Can I parasail above broken dreams?

Can I karaoke my way through the fake voices of those who scheme against me?

I just want to take a vacation from my life.

Can I hide away underneath a waterfall of awesome talents?

Can I float into the metaphors of melodies that soothe heartaches?

I just want to vacation from my life.

I want to be soothed by the songs of nature

I just want a vacation from my life

I want the horror films of my life massaged away
On a beautiful beach where ballets play

I want to lye amongst a soothing poetic breeze

Can I just take a vacation from my life?

The Other Woman

He spends late nights with her
She stimulates him
She arouses his dictation
She keeps his passions up
His pen always erect for her
Ejaculating her impressions onto
his bed of poetic passion
His heart truly belongs to her
She nurtures his spirit in ways that
I haven't been able to penetrate
I know he loves me but she has his
heart
I know he loves me but she's his
passion
I am jealous of her
No direct poetic lines for me
She has a key
While I still have to knock
I don't get holidays and weekends,
no late nights, Oh no

His pen is inside the walls of her
metaphors
His mind makes love to poetry all
night long
Caressing the body of knowledge
that sooths the soul and plays his
love songs

You see, she taps his thoughts
Rides his emotions
and
Sucks his intellect
She calls him directly while I have to call the cell between the hours of writers block and
no available mic

Loving a real poet means being the other woman

Poetry was his wife and I the other woman

Negativity, Greed and Ego

Now I have something I need to get off my chest
And if I ain't talking to you sit back relax, rest
I'm talking to the brother who strutted in here like he thought he was Kanya West

Negativity, greed and ego killed poetry
Negativity, greed and ego killed poetry

Shot it with limitations
Clubbed it with stifling situations
Stabbed it with frustration

Cut the creativity out of a passionate soul
While gasp and criticism take control

Choked by the egos of those who think more highly of themselves than they ought

Poisoned young poets passions
The complete opposite of how any creative community should be fashioned

Put their fires out with extinguishing cries of cut throat competition
While traveling on a deadly destructive mission

A mission to kill poetry

Oh you can't recite a poem now unless you get paid
Well baby you in the wrong spot because this venue is where real poets are made

A real poet does it for the love of it
A real poet ignores a garbage pit

It ain't about stroking your ego
It's about sharing your heart

It's about leaving a part of your soul on this mic
And for those of you who stepped in for a fight
Not tonight
'Cause you're in my venue now where real poets hang out
This is for all the people whose egos are fat
But your talent is like that []

Negativity, greed and ego killed poetry

Oh you don't want to sit through anyone elses set?
Did you ever think you might grow....maybe some inspiration you'll get?
Oh, excuse me you're the best poet you've ever met

Well, I stand before you to let you know
I'm a bad poet but I can always grow

Spoken Word

(beat) Spoken Word   Spoken Word
Spoken word art is rhythm, it's rhyme, it's rap, song and poetry

(beat) Spoken Word Spoken Word

It's socially conscious thoughts
It's atmosphere and mood
It's love and hate
Happiness and anger
It's history lessons
Social studies, Science
It's grooving
It's childhood memories
Playing spades and drinking Daiquiris with your girls
It's power to the people , It's empowerment
It's word jazz and sister sass, baby
Self worth and child birth
It is culture and nature and love and hate

(beat) Spoken Word Spoken Word

It's verse, word art, rune, lyrical paintings, abstract ballads, concrete satire, musical muse

(beat) Spoken Word Spoken Word

It's my form of art
And it's straight from my heart

It's word jazz

Carefully crafted word drama
It's healing through exposing trauma

It's eclectic language

Dramatic rhythms and rhymes

Old and new, bad and good times

Song sculptures that align the streets of our souls
It's melodies and verse new and old

This is the art of spoken word

The Poet

My words are my songs for my own life's encounters.. My punctuation marks define my heart ...My dialogue is satiristically smart ...My nouns, pronouns and syllables are my personal works of art

As a poet my words should create a higher altitude for adjectives. Setting your soul on fire .... These prefixes and suffixes narrate reproductive desires

Mold the idioms for my people as we climb the ladder of social freedom ...To enunciate, punctuate and define who we really are ...Remove all question marks and replace them with exclamation marks and stars

I will compound words and verbs that elevate social consciousness ...May God use me to be the author of friendly letters ...May my words extend themselves as literary ambassadors to make this world better....To forward harmonious homonyms that embrace the differences- A trend setter

May my sentences flow like a faucet of cool water bringing life where soles were dead ...May my metaphors leave their spirits fed

My duty as a poet is to speak to you ...Let you inside me to view and feel the inferno of true emotions ... Let my words and motions be the literary potions that stimulate your inner spirit with lyrics that let you know ... she feels my pain ...Passions of life's prepositions run unremittingly through my veins and what makes me a poet is my ability to touch, my compassion for people and an innate gift to capture with unique style ...the sun's smile ...an unborn child ... melodious muse for miles ... defining a new 21st century style

I am a poet ... And what I write means something to me and if it inspires and touches you .... Then I have done what a poet is suppose to do

Life

(the truth through spoken word)

Life is a series of scenes where the main character can sometimes drop their lines
Enter into horrors and lost minds
Come out in the end doing fine

Cause life is a series of scenes

Life is comedy, tragedy, drama, suspense, a love scene and agony
It is all the things you do and don't want to be
It is all the things you do and don't want to see
The director knows; he created life to be this way
And in any case you don't get to say
It's his script he wrote it
You just play the part
The obstacles aren't for you to sort

The main character is to remain steadfast and strong
While the elements sing about negative songs;
Give up! You don't have it
Maybe this isn't your thing
You're just not smart enough
You just aren't pretty enough
But baby, I'm here to say hang tough
Play the part and do each well

The no talents are the worst
They hate so hard it becomes per versed

Sit in your show and heckle you
Especially the ones you thought you knew

So when the curtain goes up and your show is performed
Think of this poem, you've been forewarned

Life is a series of scenes

Life is comedy, tragedy, drama, suspense and agony
And all the things you do and don't want to be

And that's what happens when you do your thing
Awesome talent is what you bring

But hang in there because your talent has spoken

Hang in there cause some negative spirits have been stirred

And that's what happens when the truth comes forth through spoken word

Poetic Expressions

Poetic expressions are
The voices of social consciousness
A multitude of emotions
It's metaphors of colorful oceans

An artistic painting of pictures with
words
It's bodies full of bends and swerves

It's odd shapes and twist
It's beauty a bliss

It's making love to your mind
It's complete orgasmic satisfaction where
you find

It's soothing

It's satisfying an urge or itch
It's metaphors of habits

It's word dance and movement
It's inspiring society's social
Improvement

Whether imaginary or real
It's bellowing out how you honestly feel

It's peaking senses to its ultimate high
It's giving a child his dream to fly

Poetic expressions are flowers blooming
into bouquets of beautiful ballets
It's lovers
It's making love
It's heavenly haikus from up above

Poetry is finding colors and shapes where
there aren't any
It's rhyme, song, sonnets, verse and
pantoums a plenty

Poetry is light where there's darkness

Darkness where there seems to be light
Sestinas and sonnets giving the socially blind sight

It's mountains metaphors of spoken
greeting cards
of warm wishes and poetic kisses

Mind impressions
Social sessions
Poetic expressions

Printed in the United States
96132LV00004BB/193-219/A